Yoshinobu Nozaki / Kazuko Matsumoto / Alastair Graham

SCIENCE MATTERS!

KINSEIDO

Kinseido Publishing Co., Ltd.
3-21 Kanda Jimbo-cho, Chiyoda-ku,
Tokyo 101-0051, Japan

Copyright © 2015 by Yoshinobu Nozaki
　　　　　　　　　Kazuko Matsumoto
　　　　　　　　　Alastair Graham-Marr
　　　　　　　　　Kevin Cleary

All rights reserved. No part of this publication may be reproduced, stored in a retrieval system, or transmitted, in any form or by any means, electronic, mechanical, photocopying, recording or otherwise, without the prior permission of the publisher.

First published 2015 by Kinseido Publishing Co., Ltd.

Design: parastyle inc.

音声ファイル無料ダウンロード

http://www.kinsei-do.co.jp/download/4006

この教科書で 🎧 DL 00 の表示がある箇所の音声は、上記 URL または QR コードにて無料でダウンロードできます。自習用音声としてご活用ください。

- ▶ PC からのダウンロードをお勧めします。スマートフォンなどでダウンロードされる場合は、ダウンロード前に「解凍アプリ」をインストールしてください。
- ▶ URL は、**検索ボックスではなくアドレスバー（URL 表示覧）**に入力してください。
- ▶ お使いのネットワーク環境によっては、ダウンロードできない場合があります。

◉ CD 00　左記の表示がある箇所の音声は、教室用 CD（Class Audio CD）に収録されています。

はしがき

　本書は、私たちの身近なところにトピックを求めて書き下ろした英文科学エッセイを題材に、英語力向上と科学の世界に分け入る愉しさを示す目的で制作された英語総合テキストです。エッセイの執筆者、ケヴィン・クレアリー、アラステア・グレイアム＝マー両氏は日本での豊かな教育歴を持っており、英語に美しいリズムをもたせながら、語句、構文に対する学習者への配慮が行き届いた平易な英文で読者を科学の世界に導きます。論理的展開が明快な科学エッセイならではの持ち味も十分に発揮されており、主として読解に重点を置いた学習に満足のゆく手ごたえが期待できます。

　科学の話題に事欠かない中、本書では各方面にまんべんなく目配りをして、15のトピックを選びました。太陽光を動力源に飛ぶハイテク機（Unit 1）、謎に包まれていた珍鳥のユニークな生態（Unit 2）、急速に普及する生体認証システム（Unit 4）、エレクトロニクスには不可欠の希土類元素（Unit 5）のほか、昆虫食（Unit 8）、リニアモーターカー（Unit 10）、災害救援ロボット（Unit 11）、国際宇宙ステーション（Unit 12）などが具体例です。現在を見据え、未来を展望するエッセイは、知的好奇心を刺激する迫力と魅力を備えています。

　日本語によるイントロダクションを冒頭に置いた5ページ構成の各ユニットは、本文に登場する単語に焦点を絞った予備的ドリルPre-Exercisesから始まります。

　次ページのReadingは、学習に適した400〜500ワードで完結し、スムーズな読解に役立つ語注を付けました。編集の観点から二つのパートに分けてあり、この区分は後のExercisesと連動しています。

　Readingでの学習効果を確認するExercisesには、運用力アップを狙う語法問題のFocus on Phrases、パートごとの内容を的確におさえるためのFocus on Contents、穴埋め問題を解きながらパート別要約文を完成させるSummary、そして締め括りに、手を動かして文中の重要表現や慣用表現の習得を図る作文問題Writing Practiceを配しました。切り口を変えた練習問題を通じて、多面的にエッセイの内容に迫ります。

　日常生活に科学が浸透した今日、現代人にとって、科学全般を見渡す幅広い教養は必須のものとなってきました。科学的素養は、急速に進歩する最先端テクノロジーをフォローする武器となるだけでなく、広く、論理的思考に基づき問題解決への道筋を立てる普遍的な力ともなります。本書は、科学エッセイを愉しみながら英語の実力を伸ばすことを意図した学習教材ですが、同時に、科学そのものへの関心が高まる一助となることも願っています。

この願いを常に胸に抱き、人間味あふれる語り口で幾多の優れた科学エッセイを世に送ってこられたケヴィン・クレアリー氏が、まさに本書の執筆中に急逝されたことは、著者一同にとって痛恨の極みでした。しかし、同氏の元同僚であり親しい友人でもあるグレィアム＝マー氏の温かく力強い協力の申し出により、クレアリー氏の遺志が受け継がれ、本書が完成に至ったことを、故人のご冥福を祈りつつ最後に記すこととします。

　金星堂編集部の皆様には長期にわたって多大なお力添えと励ましをいただきました。厚くお礼を申し上げます。

著者一同

本書はCheckLink（チェックリンク）対応テキストです。

CheckLinkのアイコンが表示されている設問は、CheckLinkに対応しています。CheckLinkを使用しなくても従来通りの授業ができますが、特色をご理解いただき、授業活性化のためにぜひご活用ください。

CheckLinkの特色について

大掛かりで複雑な従来のe-learningシステムとは異なり、CheckLinkのシステムは大きな特色として次の3点が挙げられます。

1. これまで行われてきた教科書を使った授業展開に大幅な変化を加えることなく、専門的な知識なしにデジタル学習環境を導入することができる。
2. PC教室やCALL教室といった最新の機器が導入された教室に限定されることなく、普通教室を使用した授業でもデジタル学習環境を導入することができる。
3. 授業中での使用に特化し、教師・学習者双方のモチベーション・集中力をアップさせ、授業自体を活性化することができる。

▶教科書を使用した授業に「デジタル学習環境」を導入できる

本システムでは、学習者は教科書のCheckLinkのアイコンが表示されている設問にPCやスマートフォン、携帯電話端末からインターネットを通して解答します。そして教師は、授業中にリアルタイムで解答結果を把握し、正解率などに応じて有効な解説を行うことができるようになっています。教科書自体は従来と何ら変わりはありません。解答の手段としてCheckLinkを使用しない場合でも、従来通りの教科書として使用して授業を行うことも、もちろん可能です。

▶教室環境を選ばない

従来の多機能なe-learning教材のように学習者側の画面に多くの機能を持たせることはせず、「解答する」ことに機能を特化しました。PCだけでなく、一部タブレット端末やスマートフォン、携帯電話端末からの解答も可能です。したがって、PC教室やCALL教室といった大掛かりな教室は必要としません。普通教室でもCheckLinkを用いた授業が可能です。教師はPCだけでなく、一部タブレット端末やスマートフォンからも解答結果の確認をすることができます。

▶授業を活性化するための支援システム

本システムは予習や復習のツールとしてではなく、授業中に活用されることで真価を発揮する仕組みになっています。CheckLinkというデジタル学習環境を通じ、教師と学習者双方が授業中に解答状況などの様々な情報を共有することで、学習者はやる気を持って解答し、教師は解答状況に応じて効果的な解説を行う、という好循環を生み出します。CheckLinkは、普段の授業をより活力のあるものへと変えていきます。

上記3つの大きな特色以外にも、掲示板などの授業中に活用できる機能を用意しています。従来通りの教科書としても使用はできますが、ぜひCheckLinkの機能をご理解いただき、普段の授業をより活性化されたものにしていくためにご活用ください。

CheckLinkの使い方

CheckLinkは、PCや一部タブレット端末、スマートフォン、携帯電話端末を用いて、この教科書のCheckLinkのアイコン表示のある設問に解答するシステムです。
・初めてCheckLinkを使う場合、以下の要領で**「学習者登録」**と**「教科書登録」**を行います。
・一度登録を済ませれば、あとは毎回**「ログイン画面」**から入るだけです。CheckLinkを使う教科書が増えたときだけ、改めて**「教科書登録」**を行ってください。

CheckLink URL

https://checklink.kinsei-do.co.jp/student/

QRコードの読み取りができる端末の場合はこちらから ▶▶▶

ご注意ください! 上記URLは**「検索ボックス」**でなく**「アドレスバー(URL表示欄)」**に入力してください。

▶学習者登録

①上記URLにアクセスすると、右のページが表示されます。学校名を入力し「ログイン画面へ」をクリックしてください。
PCの場合は「PC用はこちら」をクリックしてPC用ページを表示します。同様に学校名を入力し「ログイン画面へ」をクリックしてください。
②ログイン画面が表示されたら**「初めての方はこちら」**をクリックし「学習者登録画面」に入ります。

③自分の学籍番号、氏名、メールアドレス(学校のメールなど**PCメールを推奨**)を入力し、次に**任意のパスワード**を8桁以上20桁未満(半角英数字)で入力します。なお、学籍番号はパスワードとして使用することはできません。
④「パスワード確認」は、❸で入力したパスワードと同じものを入力します。
⑤最後に「登録」ボタンをクリックして登録は完了です。次回からは、「ログイン画面」から学籍番号とパスワードを入力してログインしてください。

▶教科書登録

①ログイン後、メニュー画面から「教科書登録」を選び（PCの場合はその後「新規登録」ボタンをクリック）、「教科書登録」画面を開きます。

②教科書と受講する授業を登録します。
教科書の最終ページにある、**教科書固有番号**のシールをはがし、印字された**16桁の数字とアルファベット**を入力します。

③授業を担当される先生から連絡された**11桁の授業ID**を入力します。

④最後に「登録」ボタンをクリックして登録は完了です。

⑤実際に使用する際は「教科書一覧」（PCの場合は「教科書選択画面」）の該当する教科書名をクリックすると、「問題解答」の画面が表示されます。

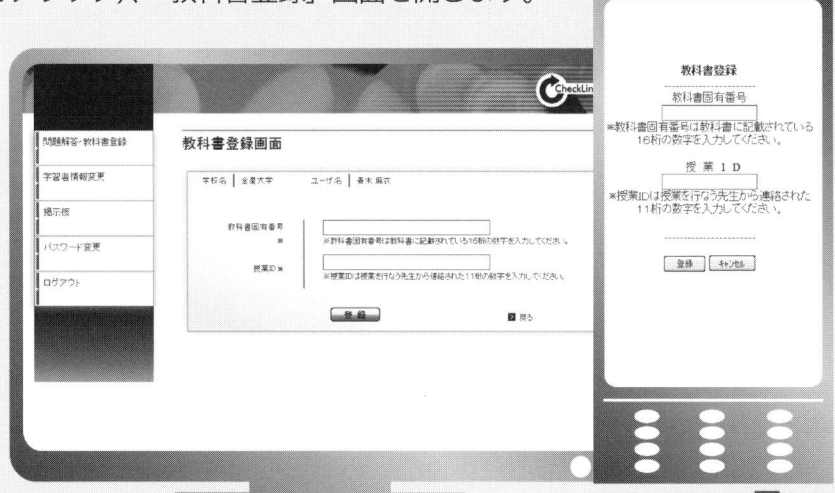

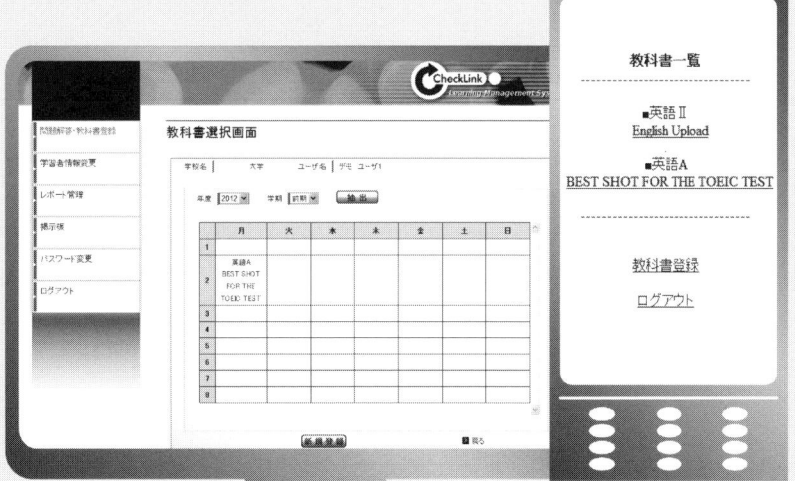

▶問題解答

①問題は教科書を見ながら解答します。この教科書の CheckLink のアイコン表示のある設問に解答できます。

②問題が表示されたら選択肢を選びます。

③表示されている問題に解答した後、「解答」ボタンをクリックすると解答が登録されます。

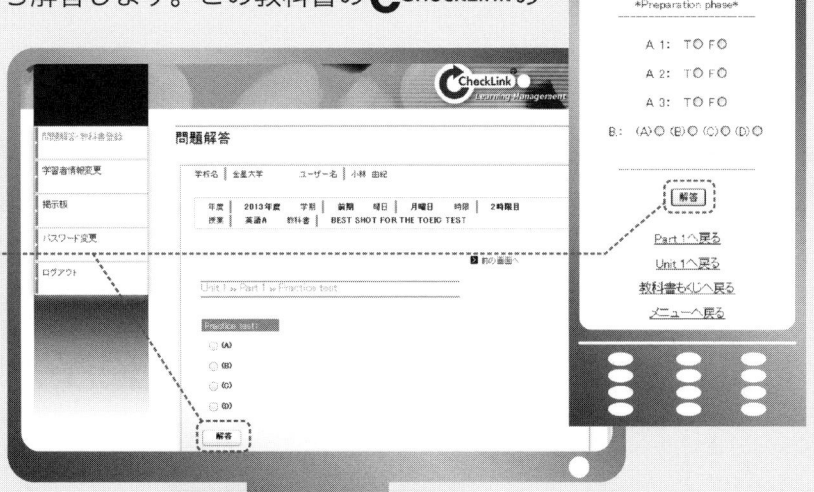

▶CheckLink 推奨環境

PC

推奨 OS
  Windows XP, Vista 以降
  Macintosh OS X 以降
  Linux

推奨ブラウザ
  Internet Explorer 6.0 以上
  Firefox 3.0 以上
  Safari
  Opera
  Google Chrome

携帯電話・スマートフォン

  3G 以降の携帯電話（docomo, au, softbank）
  iPhone, iPad
  Android OS スマートフォン、タブレット

▶CheckLink 開発

　CheckLink は奥田裕司 福岡大学教授、正興 IT ソリューション株式会社、株式会社金星堂によって共同開発されました。

　CheckLink は株式会社金星堂の登録商標です。

CheckLink の使い方に関するお問い合わせは…

正興 IT ソリューション株式会社　CheckLink 係

e-mail　checklink@seiko-denki.co.jp

Contents

Unit	Title	Subtitle	Page
Unit 1	Solar Impulse	大空を駆けるテクノロジー	11
Unit 2	The Lyrebird	美しいものまねの達人	16
Unit 3	Busy Bees	身近な働き者——ミツバチ	21
Unit 4	Biometric Data	「私」を証明するためのリスク	26
Unit 5	Rare Earth	可能性を秘めた注目の資源	31
Unit 6	Herd Immunity	集団感染のリスクを減らすには	36
Unit 7	Geothermal Energy	安定した電力源としての可能性	41
Unit 8	Insects for Food	豊富で栄養価の高い身近な食材	46
Unit 9	Ivory	象牙取引の現実	51
Unit 10	Maglev Train	疾走する未来のトレイン	56
Unit 11	Robots	活躍の場を広げるロボット	61
Unit 12	International Space Station	約400キロ上空の実験施設	66
Unit 13	Pipe Organ	技術が生み出す多彩な音色	71
Unit 14	Earthquake and Detection Systems	命を守るテクノロジー	76
Unit 15	Abyss	生命を育む熱水噴出孔	81

[写真提供一覧]

▶株式会社テムザック(p61、p63)
▶JAXA / NASA(p68)
▶JAMSTEC(p81、p83)
▶時事通信フォト(p28、p33、p58、p78)
▶シンドラーエレベータ株式会社(p11、p13)

※アイウエオ順。( )は掲載ページ

Solar Impulse
大空を駆けるテクノロジー

Unit 1

太陽光エネルギーだけで飛ぶソーラーインパルスは、開発から約10年でアメリカ横断飛行を達成しました。各航空会社が飛行時間短縮に目の色を変える中、ソーラーインパルスはスピードを度外視し、再生可能エネルギーを活用したクリーンなフライトの実現に力を注ぎます。太陽電池の改良や機体デザインの工夫といったテクノロジー面でのチャレンジと、パイロットの冒険精神が呼応した同機は航空業界に革命を起こすかもしれません。

Pre-Exercises

Focus on Words

日本語の意味に合うようにa～f、g～lの各語群から適切な語を選びましょう。

1. 夜間飛行を楽しむ　　　　　　　　　enjoy a night (　　)
2. 大気汚染に苦しむ　　　　　　　　　suffer from air (　　)
3. 生物学的特徴を分析する　　　　　　analyze a biological (　　)
4. 燃料不足に直面する　　　　　　　　face a (　　) shortage
5. ある装置を操作する　　　　　　　　operate a (　　)

> **a.** feature　**b.** flight　**c.** fuel
> **d.** pollution　**e.** device　**f.** satellite

6. 太陽熱暖房を利用する　　　　　　　use (　　) heating
7. 人を奮い立たせるスピーチをする　　make an (　　) speech
8. 高度情報システムに頼る　　　　　　rely on (　　) information systems
9. 効率的なエネルギー技術を開発する　develop an (　　) energy technology
10. 曇り空を見る　　　　　　　　　　look at a (　　) sky

> **g.** advanced　**h.** cloudy　**i.** efficient
> **j.** inspiring　**k.** solar　**l.** angled

Reading

Part I

Using a jet, people can go from San Francisco to New York City in about six hours. So what could be so exciting about a new plane, Solar Impulse, that took over two months to fly between those two cities? Two words: clean energy. By using solar energy, the flight required no fuel, and it produced no pollution. But the cross-country flight did create a lot of excitement.

Swiss pioneers Bertrand Piccard, a psychiatrist and balloonist and André Borschberg, an engineer, entrepreneur and professional pilot started working on Solar Impulse in 2003. A team of about 50 experts brought the plane to the point where it could successfully fly, for the first time in history, day and night powered only by the sun and across the USA in 2013. As the plane carries only one person—the pilot—it is not meant to replace a passenger jet aircraft.

Instead, it is intended to show a new way of using renewable energy. The cross-country trip took two months because Solar Impulse visited many cities on the way from the West Coast to the East Coast. Many people were excited to get a close look at the inspiring plane that flies for free, and perhaps they caught a glimpse of a brighter future, too.

Part II

The elegant plane's wings are nearly three times as long as its body. One reason for its 63.4 meter wingspan is to give the plane enough surface area to capture the necessary amount of sunlight.

Another reason for the long wings is to give the airplane

enough "lift" to fly. Although it goes only 70 km/h, the amount of air going under the long, angled wings pushes up on them enough to keep the airplane aloft.

A key feature of the high-tech plane is its energy storage system, which consists of extremely advanced lithium-polymer batteries. These batteries are charged up by the solar panels that cover Solar Impulse's wings and convert sunlight to electricity.

As you may imagine, the plane's battery-powered engines are very efficient. Amazingly, Solar Impulse produces more energy than it uses. Thus, the plane can keep flying even when it is cloudy or dark.

The combination of technologies that allows Solar Impulse to travel without stopping for fuel has great promise. For example, low-flying satellites, weather monitoring devices, and perhaps flying electricity generators will use the technology that the Solar Impulse team has developed. Solar Impulse won't set any speed records and yet, of course, it will help accelerate us into an age of clean energy.

(423 words)

■機体（HB-SIA※）について

- ■主翼長＝63.4 m
- ■機体長＝21.85 m
- ■機体高＝6.4 m
- ■機体重量＝1600 kg
- ■平均飛行速度＝70 km/h
- ■最高高度＝8500 m

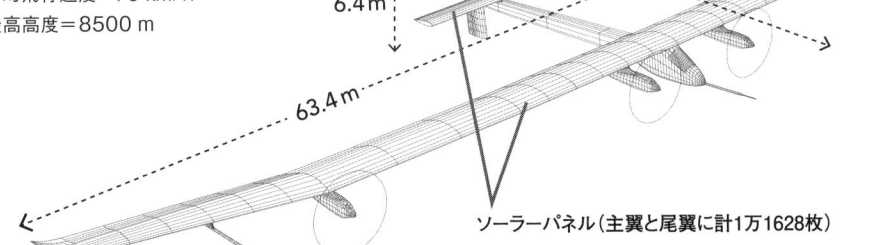

※最初の試作機であり、これで米国主要都市訪問や大陸横断飛行に成功した。より長距離・長時間の飛行が可能な改良版、HB-SIBも開発された。

Exercises

Focus on Phrases

語群から（　）に適切な語を入れて英文を完成させましょう。
その際、必要に応じて語形は変えること。

1. The newly-formed team of engineers started to (　　　　) on a secret project.
2. While I was hiking in the forest, I (　　　　) a glimpse of an unusual bird.
3. The function of a battery is to (　　　　) chemical energy into electrical energy.
4. The committee will (　　　　) of five members at first, but more people may be added later.
5. A Swiss swimmer (　　　　) the world record yesterday.

catch　consist　convert　set　work

Focus on Contents

本文の内容に合うように（　）に適切な語句を選びましょう。

Part I

1. Solar Impulse is a success story for (　) engineering.
   a. cross-country　b. jet-propelled　c. pollution-free
2. The importance of Solar Impulse is that it (　　).
   a. carries many passengers　b. uses a newly developed fuel
   c. uses renewable energy

Part II

1. (　) are needed to keep a solar plane in the air when it is dark or cloudy.
   a. Cloth-covered wings　b. Super-efficient batteries
   c. Highly-reflective panels
2. Solar Impulse has long wings so that it can (　　).
   a. capture enough sunlight　b. ensure a non-stop flight
   c. resist strong winds

Solar Impulse   Unit 1

Summary

（　）にa〜eから適切な語を選び、それぞれのPartの要約文を作りましょう。

Part I   DL 04   CD1-04

Solar Impulse does not create pollution, but it does (1.　) a great deal of excitement. On its first trip (2.　) the United States it stopped at many cities. Crowds (3.　) to see the plane. They understood that the plane was meant to (4.　) a message about clean energy, not passengers.

a. across   **b.** between   **c.** carry   **d.** cause   **e.** gathered

Part II   DL 05   CD1-05

Solar Impulse has extremely long wings. They are covered with solar panels, which (1.　) sunlight into electricity. The electricity is used to (2.　) the plane's batteries, which power the plane's engines. As a result, Solar Impulse can fly when it is cloudy or dark. In fact, Solar Impulse (3.　) more energy than it uses. The technology (4.　) for the plane will help us move away from using fossil fuels for energy.

a. advanced   **b.** charge   **c.** convert   **d.** creates   **e.** developed

Writing Practice

日本文の意味に合った英文になるように、[　]内の語句を並べかえましょう。

1. ソーラーインパルスは、なぜ胴体の3倍もの長さの翼をもっているのだろうか。

   Why does Solar Impulse have wings [are / as long as / its body / three times / that]?

   _____

   _____

2. 一つの理由は、翼長が、低速でも機体を飛行させるのに十分な揚力を生み出すからだ。

   One reason is that the wingspan [allows / enough lift / to create / to fly / the plane] in spite of its low speed.

   _____

   _____

15

Unit 2

The Lyrebird
美しいものまねの達人

オーストラリアの10セント硬貨を飾るコトドリ。近年、この珍鳥のユニークな習性がわかってきました。コアラの鳴き声や水が滴る音、さらには無機質な機械音まで巧みに再現できるこのものまねの名手は、さえずるのも得意ならばダンスをするのも上手です。オスは竪琴 (lyre) に似た立派な飾り羽を優雅に操り、歌と踊りを盛り込んだ魅惑的なパフォーマンスでメスのハートを射止めにかかります。

Pre-Exercises

Focus on Words

CheckLink

日本語の意味に合うようにa～f、g～lの各語群から適切な語を選びましょう。

1. かごに入れて鳥を飼う　　keep birds in (　　)
2. 宗教儀式を行う　　perform a religious (　　)
3. 芸術的な才能を示す　　show artistic (　　)
4. 決まったやり方を覚える　　learn the (　　)
5. シドニーの親戚を訪ねる　　visit (　　) in Sydney

a. routines　**b.** captivity　**c.** flourish
d. ritual　**e.** abilities　**f.** relatives

6. 個々の質問に答える　　answer (　　) questions
7. 独立した生活を送る　　live an (　　) life
8. 生きたブタを売る　　sell (　　) pigs
9. 驚くべき発見をする　　make an (　　) discovery
10. 城の外壁を建てる　　build the (　　) walls of the castle

g. amazing　**h.** coordinated　**i.** live
j. individual　**k.** independent　**l.** outer

Reading

Part I

If you have been to Australia, you have surely seen a lyrebird, at least as an image on the Australian 10 cent coin. But it would be much better to see—and hear—a live lyrebird in action.

In the wild, the lyrebird is extremely shy. Researchers are rarely able to catch sight of lyrebirds, let alone capture them for study. Making things worse, lyrebirds that are captured usually don't reproduce in captivity. Fortunately for science and animal lovers, however, one population of the bird in Australia has lost its fear of humans, which has allowed scientists to learn a lot about this master mimic.

In addition to being able to imitate nearly any sound it hears, another of the lyrebird's claims to fame is its courting ritual. The male builds a stage, on which he performs a very complicated song-and-dance routine. Unique in the animal world, the lyrebird's songs and dances are independent elements that are intentionally combined in creative ways.

Part II

In addition to imitations of other birds and sounds from its environment, such as koalas or water drops falling into a pool, the songs of the lyrebird include hums, clicks, thrills, and buzzes. The dance steps feature strutting, stomping, and hopping, all with coordinated body movements.

Finally, the songs and dances are continually updated and are combined in new ways. It takes years for a lyrebird to develop an individual set of routines that will impress lady lyrebirds.

The lyrebird was named after the lyre, but not because of the bird's amazing musical abilities. Instead, the name comes from the way it extends its tail feathers in a canopy over its head. The two outer feathers make S curves, and the other feathers spread apart in a web between them, creating a 1.5-meter wide lyre-shaped canopy. This canopy is sometimes displayed throughout a part of a dance, or as a final flourish.

In fact, a male lyrebird's tail is 70% of its one-meter body length. Partly because of its long, heavy tail, and also due to its short, weak wings, one thing the bird cannot do very well is fly. To go up a tree, a lyrebird uses its strong legs to jump up to tree branches, and then it climbs and hops to get to its roost.

The lyrebird does use its wings, but only to glide from a high point to the ground. It seems that flying ability is the only way it can't imitate its aerodynamically-gifted relatives.

(412 words)

extend 十分に伸ばす
canopy 天蓋
in a web
（クモの巣状に）複雑に絡み合って

flourish 派手な身振り

branches 枝
roost 止まり木
glide from ~ to ...
～から…へ移動する
aerodynamically-gifted
空気力学的に能力に恵まれた
relatives
同族の動物（この場合は鳥類）

▶ 求愛をしているオスのコトドリ。

▶ オスのコトドリをモチーフにしたオーストラリア10セント硬貨（裏面）。

Exercises

Focus on Phrases

語群から（　）に適切な語を入れて英文を完成させましょう。
その際、必要に応じて語形は変えること。

1. I saw a rabbit (　　　　　) into a hole.
2. The satellite was (　　　　　) after a famous astronomer.
3. The soldier stood with his feet (　　　　　) apart.
4. I caught (　　　　　) of Mt. Fuji from the bullet train window.
5. The accident must have (　　　　　) from his lack of attention.

sight   fall   name   come   spread

Focus on Contents

本文の内容に合うように（　）に適切な語句を選びましょう。

Part I

1. Some lyrebirds in Australia gave scientists chances to learn about their (　　).
   a. beautiful songs　b. favorite food　c. mimic performance
2. (　　) birds combine songs and dances in courting behavior.
   a. Few　b. Many　c. All

Part II

1. The name of the lyrebird comes from its (　　).
   a. body size　b. singing abilities　c. physical feature
2. Lyrebird is (　　) an expert at flying.
   a. far from　b. nothing but　c. more than

Summary

（　）にa〜eから適切な語を選び、それぞれのPartの要約文を作りましょう。

Part I

　The lyrebird, found in Australia, is a very (1.　) creature, and it is rather hard for people to approach them, so, very few of their behaviors were known to scientists. However, one group of the birds that did not (2.　) humans allowed us to learn a lot about their unique ability to imitate various sounds. The lyrebird is really a master (3.　) in the wild. Another notable feature of the lyrebird is its (4.　) dance performance.

a. attack　**b.** complicated　**c.** fear　**d.** shy　**e.** mimic

Part II

　The lyrebird imitates any sound both natural and artificial. Interestingly, they (1.　) their songs with impressive dances using their beautiful tail feathers. During the dance performance, the male lyrebird's long tail will (2.　) in a lyre-shaped canopy, which gave the bird its name. The "lyre" they display will be as wide as 1.5 meters. However, (3.　) to its long, heavy tail, the lyrebird cannot fly very well; it just (4.　) from up high.

a. combine　**b.** due　**c.** extend　**d.** fly　**e.** glides

Writing Practice

日本文の意味に合った英文になるように、[　]内の語句を並べかえましょう。

1. コトドリの自慢の一つは、耳にする音を、ほぼ何であれ真似することだ。
   [claims / fame / lyrebird's / of / one / the / to] is mimicking almost whatever sound it hears.

2. コトドリが、メスを引きつけるダンスを身につけるには何年もかかる。
   [a lyrebird / develop / for / it / takes / to / years] a dance that will attract females.

20

Unit 3

Busy Bees
身近な働き者——ミツバチ

子孫を残そうとする草花にとっても、ハチミツ好きの人間にとっても、ミツバチは大切なパートナーです。"busy as a bee"という慣用句が生まれるほどよく働くこのミツバチの命が現在、人間によって脅かされています。各地で起こる「ミツバチ一斉失踪事件」の真相はいまだに解明されていませんが、散布された農薬との関係が疑われています。人間による過酷なハチミツ収集によって、本来備わっているはずの免疫力を低下させた可能性も否定できません。

Pre-Exercises

Focus on Words

日本語の意味に合うようにa〜f、g〜lの各語群から適切な語を選びましょう。

1. 作物の植え付けをする　　　plant a (　　)
2. 花粉を作る　　　　　　　　produce (　　)
3. 供給を限定する　　　　　　restrict (　　)
4. 被害者の身元を確認する　　identify the (　　)
5. 殺虫剤を散布する　　　　　spray (　　)

　　　a. crop　　**b.** colony　　**c.** pollen
　　　d. supply　　**e.** victim　　**f.** pesticide

6. よくある病気にかかる　　　catch a (　　) disease
7. 有益な取引をする　　　　　make a (　　) deal
8. 主要な原因を突き止める　　find out the (　　) cause
9. 農業開発を促進する　　　　promote (　　) development
10. 勤勉な学生を表彰する　　　give awards to (　　) students

　　　g. agricultural　　**h.** beneficial　　**i.** common
　　　j. destructive　　**k.** hard-working　　**l.** prime

Reading

Part I

Have you ever heard the expression, "busy as a bee"? Bees are indeed very busy, and not just in making honey. We have bees to thank for much of the food that we enjoy. Every year, hard-working bees go from field to field, pollinating crops. Many plants need to have pollen from one flower go to another flower so that they can produce seeds and reproduce.

Although the wind can blow pollen to a waiting flower, this method relies completely on chance. Birds, hummingbirds, spiders, and other animals might visit different flowers, and end up pollinating plants by accident. Beetles are the most common pollinators worldwide, but they are destructive to plants, too. Commercial farming requires safe and efficient production in order to be profitable. Hence, the bees.

Every spring, beekeepers take hives that contain thousands or millions of bees to a farmer's field, let the bees loose, and watch as they go from flower to flower. The bees are happy as they collect nectar from the flowers for energy and pollen to bring back to the hive, where it is used as food for the bee larvae. As the bees visit the flowers in the fields or on the trees, they inadvertently deposit pollen just where it is needed. Without bee-assisted pollination, almonds, blueberries, and apples would be in very short supply.

Part II

Bees and flowers have evolved together to create a mutually beneficial pollination system. For example, the bees have long snouts that allow them to pick up the pollen

Notes

"busy as a bee"
「多忙を極める」(慣用句)

pollinating crops
農作物に受粉して
pollinate は「〜に受粉する」という意味。

pollen 花粉
p.22 l.12 の pollinator は「(鳥や昆虫などの)受粉媒介者」

chance 運

hummingbirds
ハチドリ

end up 〜
結局〜することになる

beetles 甲虫
鞘翅目の昆虫の総称

hives ミツバチの巣箱

let the bees loose
ミツバチを解き放つ

nectar 花の蜜

larvae 幼虫
larva の複数形

inadvertently
意図せずに

very short supply
たいへんな供給不足

mutually beneficial
相互に利益をもたらす

snout (昆虫の)口先

in the male reproductive organs, called the anthers, and then deposit the pollen in the female reproductive organs, called the stigma, as it feeds on each flower. For their part, flowers have bright colors and useful shapes to attract and encourage bees to drop by for a meal.

Unfortunately, the number of bees has been decreasing recently. Entire colonies are being wiped out, victims of a "colony collapse disorder." It is not clear what is causing this destruction, but a prime suspect is the neonicotinoids used in many pesticides. Perhaps the stress of their working life, as well as exposure to agricultural chemicals, has weakened bees' natural immunity so much that they have trouble fighting off the chemicals, viruses, fungi, and bacteria that they would normally survive.

In any case, with a decreasing number of bees and an increasing amount of food production, we are asking the bees to be more industrious than ever before. Thus, for the sake of our food supply, we need to find a way to protect our hard-working honey producers.

(426 words)

▶ ネオニコチノイド系農薬を禁止する動きは世界中に広がりつつある。2013年、EUでは加盟国全域で2年間の使用を原則禁止にした。

Exercises

Focus on Phrases

語群から ( ) に適切な語を入れて英文を完成させましょう。
その際、必要に応じて語形は変えること。

1. We prepared some plastic bags so that party guests could (　　　　　) back food to their home.
2. She advised us not to (　　　　　) on computers too much.
3. The severe drought has (　　　　　) out our crops this year.
4. I was so happy to sit next to her, but (　　　　　) up saying nothing at all.
5. My brother will (　　　　　) by my office to give me a birthday gift.

bring   drop   end   rely   wipe

Focus on Contents

本文の内容に合うように ( ) に適切な語句を選びましょう。

Part I

1. The pollination of flowers by the wind can be (　　).
   a. unreliable   **b.** profitable   **c.** destructive
2. Visiting flowers, bees unknowingly place (　　) in the right spot.
   a. hives   **b.** larvae   **c.** pollen

Part II

1. Bees are easily attracted by the (　　) of flowers.
   a. fruity smells   **b.** modern shapes   **c.** vivid colors
2. It is highly possible that a "colony collapse disorder" has been caused by (　　).
   a. fungi   **b.** neonicotinoids   **c.** virus

Busy Bees Unit 3

Summary

(　)にa～eから適切な語を選び、それぞれのPartの要約文を作りましょう。

Part I

Typically, plants need to have pollen so that they can (1.　) fruits or seeds. Some plants have the pollen they need brought by the wind, and others get it via beetles, spiders or birds. However, the most reliable method of pollination is to let bees (2.　) pollen. Unlike beetles, bees are the least (3.　) to the plants. Thus, bee-assisted pollination guarantees safe and (4.　) production for commercial farming.

a. collect　**b.** destructive　**c.** efficient　**d.** produce　**e.** world-wide

Part II

Bees and flowers have (1.　) a mutually beneficial cooperation through their long evolution. (2.　) by bright colors of flowers, and feeding on them, bees pick up and carry pollen from anthers to stigmas. Recently, however, bee colonies are being (3.　) out. It is suspected that their immune system has been (4.　) by chemicals contained in agricultural pesticides. We humans must take some steps to protect bees for the sake of our food supply.

a. attracted　**b.** created　**c.** survived　**d.** weakened　**e.** wiped

Writing Practice

日本文の意味に合った英文になるように、[　]内の語句を並べかえましょう。

1. もしハチが花の受粉を行わなかったら、多くの果物の供給は非常に乏しくなるだろう。
   If flowers were not pollinated by bees, many fruits [short / in / be / supply / very / would].

2. 免疫力がひどく弱まったので、ハチは、有害なウイルスを撃退するのが困難になった。
   The immunity of bees has weakened [fighting off / have / so much / they / that / trouble] harmful viruses.

Unit 4

Biometric Data
「私」を証明するためのリスク

かつてはSFの中でしか見られなかった生体認証の実用化が急ピッチで進んでいます。銀行のATMや情報端末のログインで使われる指紋認証や静脈認証は、日常生活にすっかり浸透しているようです。生体認証の大きな魅力のひとつはセキュリティレベルの高さにあります。しかし本当に安全と言い切れるのでしょうか。残念ながら、機械の誤作動や悪意持つ第三者による情報操作によるトラブルも、SFの世界から現実界へと移行しています。

Pre-Exercises

Focus on Words

日本語の意味に合うようにa〜f、g〜lの各語群から適切な語を選びましょう。

1. 指令を撤回する　　　　　　withdraw a (　　)
2. ビーッという音を立てる　　make a (　　)
3. 検査官を任命する　　　　　appoint an (　　)
4. モニターの解像度を変える　change the monitor's (　　)
5. 犯罪者を罰する　　　　　　punish a (　　)

> **a.** access　**b.** beep　**c.** command
> **d.** resolution　**e.** inspector　**f.** criminal

6. 無線機器を操作する　　　　operate a (　　) device
7. 独特な味を楽しむ　　　　　enjoy a (　　) flavor
8. 顔の表情を観察する　　　　observe (　　) expressions
9. 肯定的な反応を示す　　　　have a (　　) reaction
10. 政治的リーダーシップを示す　demonstrate (　　) leadership

> **g.** convenient　**h.** facial　**i.** political
> **j.** positive　**k.** wireless　**l.** unique

Reading

Part I

The traveler approaches the machine. He opens a small booklet, and inserts it into a slot. He is then told to press his two index fingers onto two lit-up pads. The next command is to lift his fingers and look at a blue circle. After a beep, the blue circle disappears, the machine prints out a slip of paper, and the traveler is instructed to gather his booklet and go through the gate. As he approaches, the gate's doors automatically open.

Until recently, the above scene would have been considered a scene from science fiction. Today, millions of travelers are able to enter or leave their country without needing to talk to a border guard or an immigration inspector. All they have to do is use an e-passport.

What happens inside the machine? First, when the passport is inserted into the slot, a scanner picks up a code from the machine readable zone of the data page. Next, a wireless network connection is made with the data chip that is embedded in the passport. The scanned code provides a key that unlocks access to the chip. The chip then sends a stream of data to the border control machine.

When the traveler presses his fingers on the pads, his unique fingerprint pattern is read and sent to a database. If the prints match the ones on record for that person, an OK signal is returned to the machine. If they do not match, or it is found that the person is someone that the government wants to talk to, then the border control supervisor's machine is notified, and the traveler is asked to have an interview.

Notes

booklet 小冊子
index fingers （両手の）人差し指
lit-up 光で照らされた
beep ビープ音（ピーッという音）
gather ~ ～を引き寄せる

border guard 国境警備員
immigration inspector 入国管理検査官

is embedded in ~ ～に埋め込まれている

a stream of data 続々と出てくるデータ

fingerprint pattern 指紋の模様

border control supervisor's 出入国管理者の
interview 面談

Part II

What about the camera? The stream of data from the chip in the passport includes the photograph that is on the data page, in high resolution. The images from the passport and the camera are compared using facial recognition software.

Again, if there is a match, all is well and the traveler is one step closer to going through the border. But if the system cannot verify the traveler, or if the image matches a person of interest, then a supervisor is notified and the traveler is detained for an interview.

This system is very convenient, isn't it? However, what if the software mistakenly identifies you as a dangerous criminal? What if someone puts a note onto your records that indicates you are a troublemaker? To be sure, your biometrics, or unique identification data, enables you to identify yourself speedily enough when needed.

Unfortunately, however, this positive identification also makes it possible for a government to harass people who are seen as problems because of their political views or for other reasons. Also, a criminal who somehow gains access to your biometrics might be able to steal your identity. Convenience always comes with a price. (471 words)

▶日本でも成田や関西空港などで、生体認証による搭乗手続きが導入されている。

Exercises

Focus on Phrases

語群から（　）に適切な語を入れて英文を完成させましょう。
その際、必要に応じて語形は変えること。

1. Her English is so fluent that I mistakenly (　　　　　) her as an English native speaker.
2. After a two-year childcare leave, my wife (　　　　　) to a full-time job.
3. All the set lunch menus here used to (　　　　　) with soup.
4. Just before (　　　　　) through customs, the man was arrested.
5. I (　　　　　) a DVD into the Multiple-Drive, but nothing happened.

come　go　identify　insert　return

Focus on Contents

本文の内容に合うように（　）に適切な語句を選びましょう。

Part I

1. Today, travelers having (　) can skip the interview with a border guard.
   a. an e-passport　**b.** a scanning machine　**c.** a wireless network
2. (　) travelers' fingerprints match the ones on their record, the airport authorities will question them.
   a. Besides　**b.** However　**c.** Unless

Part II

1. Facial recognition (　) will detect a traveler's cheating.
   a. slot　**b.** expert　**c.** software
2. There are (　) of biometric data abuses by governments and criminals.
   a. archives　**b.** laws　**c.** risks

Summary

( )にa～eから適切な語を選び、それぞれのPartの要約文を作りましょう。

Part I

As in an SF film, travelers with their e-passports can easily cross the border or go through the gate to the plane without any check by a guard or an (1.). All that is needed is biometric data embedded in the passport. First, a scanner picks up a (2.) from the page, which allows the border (3.) machine to read all the necessary data and check your (4.).

a. code　**b.** control　**c.** fingerprints　**d.** inspector　**e.** views

Part II

The data chip includes your picture so that the facial (1.) software can compare the images from the passport and the camera. If the system doesn't (2.) the traveler, he/she may be interviewed personally by a supervisor. It is true that biometric identification is (3.), but it is not impossible for somebody to make bad use of your data. Biometric identification does accurately identify people, but it does not come without a (4.).

a. convenient　**b.** price　**c.** recognition　**d.** resolution　**e.** verify

Writing Practice

日本文の意味に合った英文になるように、[ ]内の語句を並べかえましょう。

1. スキャンされた暗号が、あなたの指紋を機械で読み取るのを可能にする解法を与えてくれる。
   The scanned code provides [a key / allows / read / that / the machine / to] your fingerprints.

2. もし誰かが、あなたの身分を悪用する目的で、生体認証のデータを入手したらどうなるだろう。
   [access / gains / if / someone / to / what] your biometric data in order to abuse your identity?

Unit 5

Rare Earth
可能性を秘めた注目の資源

2012年、南鳥島付近にレアアースの鉱床が発見されたというニュースは朗報として伝えられました。名前とは裏腹に、液晶ディスプレイの電極に使われるインジウムのように産出量の多い物質がある一方、たとえばウィンドタービンのマグネットに利用されるテルビウムやジスプロシウムのように産出地域が限られた物質も多くあります。後者の場合、一国への依存を避けるための方策が必要です。国家間の争いの火種にもなりかねないレアアース問題は深刻さを増しています。

Pre-Exercises

Focus on Words

日本語の意味に合うようにa～f、g～lの各語群から適切な語を選びましょう。

1. 放射性元素を取り除く　　　　remove the radioactive (　　)
2. 経済的需要を生み出す　　　　generate economic (　　)
3. 天然資源を利用する　　　　　utilize natural (　　)
4. 将来性を持つ　　　　　　　　hold (　　) for the future
5. その問題の解決策を見出す　　work out a (　　) to a problem

> **a.** demand **b.** element **c.** promise
> **d.** resources **e.** smelter **f.** solution

6. 携帯型キーボードを取りつける　set up a (　　) keyboard
7. 大量の証拠を見つける　　　　　find (　　) evidence
8. 貴重な時間を節約する　　　　　save (　　) time
9. 代理の教員として働く　　　　　work as a (　　) teacher
10. 限られた資金を配分する　　　　allocate (　　) funds

> **g.** abundant **h.** extracted **i.** limited
> **j.** mobile **k.** precious **l.** substitute

Reading

Part I

Solar cells, wind turbine magnets, LCD screens, mobile phones, highly-advanced radar systems, X-ray units, electric cars—these and many other products that our society depends on in turn rely on unique metals known as "rare earths." If our supply of these metals were to be interrupted, we'd have to do without many of the products that define modern life, or which promise us a more environmentally-friendly future.

The seventeen elements that are known as rare earths are actually common in the Earth's crust. They are "rare" only because they are not in concentrated portions. Thus, a large amount of a base metal or a base material, such as clay, has to be processed to yield the desired metals.

For example, indium often occurs with zinc. In order to isolate indium, the material leftover from zinc production has to be reprocessed. In the past, the cost of isolating indium, including transporting the base material to a capable smelter, was much higher than the value of the resulting extracted metal. These days, improved smelters can efficiently, and cost-effectively, extract indium.

Since this rare earth is essential for production of LCD TVs, mobile phone screens, and solar cells, demand for it has increased significantly. As a result, the price has gone up as well, and processes to recover indium that were once too expensive now make sense economically.

Part II

Indium is produced in several countries. However, most other rare earths have a much more limited supply. For example, the magnets in wind turbines depend on

Notes

wind turbine magnets 風力タービン用磁石
LCD screens 液晶ディスプレイ画面 LCDはLiquid Crystal Displayの略
X-ray units X線装置
in turn こちらは今度は
define ~ ~を特徴づける

Earth's crust 地殻
concentrated portions 集中した部分
base metal 卑金属（空中で容易に酸化されやすく、水分・二酸化炭素などによって侵されやすい金属。鉄、銅、鉛など）
indium インジウム
occur （動植物・鉱物が）見出される
zinc 亜鉛
leftover 残り
smelter 製錬所
resulting extracted metal 結果として抽出された金属

terbium and dysprosium, and these two rare earths are only available from China. In fact, China supplies almost all of the rare earths used today. China has abundant supplies of these metals, and the factories that use them are often there as well.

To avoid dependence on one country for these precious resources, several approaches are being taken. First, mines are being opened up in resource-rich countries, such as Australia, Brazil, Canada, and Russia.

Secondly, efforts are being made to recover rare earths from existing sources, such as slag piles and used electronics. A longer-term solution is to lessen the need for them, for example by designing products that use substitute materials. Several nanomaterials in development show promise of being able to replace rare earths.

In the short term, rare earths have limited availability and a high price. With time, there will be many more sources for these currently essential, yet expensive to extract, metals.

(406 words)

▶ 2012年、東京大学の研究チームは南鳥島周辺の海底にレアアースが大量に（日本の1年の消費量の約230倍）埋蔵されていると発表した。以後、科学技術庁が将来の商用化を目指して本格的な調査に乗り出したが、開発コストとの費用対効果が割に合わないと批判的な意見も出ている。

Exercises

Focus on Phrases

語群から（　）に適切な語を入れて英文を完成させましょう。
その際、必要に応じて語形は変えること。

1. Because of the severe winter, our electricity costs (　　　　) up last February.
2. It might be risky to (　　　　) too much on digital technology.
3. I'm afraid that your story doesn't (　　　　) sense.
4. Our boss never fails to (　　　　) a balanced approach to complicated matters.
5. Their research will (　　　　) up a new field of biology.

> depend　go　make　take　open

Focus on Contents

本文の内容に合うように（　）に適切な語句を選びましょう。

Part I

1. Despite their names, rare earths are (　) in the Earth's crust.
   a. actual　b. common　c. exceptional
2. In the past, extracting indium from zinc took (　) than now.
   a. less energy　b. higher risk　c. more money

Part II

1. Some rare earths are almost (　) produced in China.
   a. exclusively　b. hardly　c. unexpectedly
2. In future, (　) will be used as a replacement for rare earths.
   a. electronics devices　b. nanomaterial　c. natural resources

Rare Earth   Unit 5

Summary

( ) に a～e から適切な語を選び、それぞれの Part の要約文を作りましょう。

Part I   DL 20   CD1-20

Rare earths are indispensable in modern life. If their supply were to be (1.), we could not have the benefits of so many highly-advanced products. However, rare earths, indium for example, are not (2.) in specific places but widely spread in the Earth's crust, making them hard to (3.). We need (4.) smelters in order to yield these precious metals.

a. concentrated   **b.** extract   **c.** improved   **d.** interrupted   **e.** transport

Part II   DL 21   CD1-21

Today, China has (1.) supplies of many rare earths, but other countries generally have very (2.) resources of these metals. If we are to stop relying on one country for such resources, we should not only open new mines, but also recycle the (3.) metals that have been used in electronics, for instance. Also, for a long term solution, (4.) materials need to be developed to replace rare earths.

a. abundant   **b.** essential   **c.** existing   **d.** limited   **e.** substitute

Writing Practice

日本文の意味に合った英文になるように、[　]内の語句を並べかえましょう。

1. 以前は、インジウムを分離する工程はとても高くついたので、経済的には意味がなかった。
   In the past, the process to isolate indium [cost / make / much / sense / to / too] economically.

2. レアアースの供給を一カ国だけに頼るのを避けるため、各国はいろいろな対策を試みている。
   Countries have tried to [approaches / avoid / dependence / on / take / to] one country for the supply of rare earths.

Unit 6

Herd Immunity
集団感染のリスクを減らすには

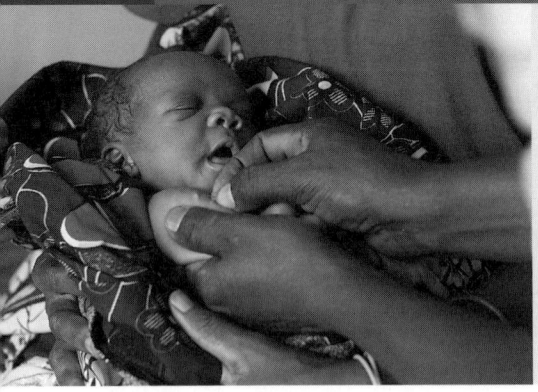

猛威を振るう伝染病の恐怖は広く知られています。ひとたび蔓延すると手がつけられなくなり、村落の半数以上がわずか数日のうちに犠牲になった例も珍しくありません。集団予防接種は、この惨状を回避するための有効手段として考えられ、また実際に高い効果を上げてきました。しかし近年、副作用を恐れて我が子への接種を拒む親が増えています。集団感染を招くことになりかねないこの状況を変えるには、接種に対する正しい情報の伝達が必須です。

Pre-Exercises

Focus on Words

日本語の意味に合うようにa～f、g～lの各語群から適切な語を選びましょう。

1. 病気の発生を防ぐ　　　　　prevent an (　　) of disease
2. 村人全員と知り合いになる　　get to know all the (　　)
3. 穴居人の遺物を発見する　　　find remains of cave (　　)
4. 衛生状態の向上を促進する　　promote better (　　)
5. 生存の可能性を高める　　　　increase the (　　) of survival

> **a.** chances　**b.** dwellers　**c.** hygiene
> **d.** immunity　**e.** outbreak　**f.** villagers

6. か弱い子供たちを守る　　　　protect (　　) children
7. 地球規模の問題を扱う　　　　deal with (　　) issues
8. アルバイトを探す　　　　　　look for a (　　) job
9. 信頼できない人を避ける　　　avoid an (　　) person
10. 政府の指針に反対する　　　　disagree with (　　) guidelines

> **g.** interconnected　**h.** governmental　**i.** global
> **j.** side　**k.** unreliable　**l.** vulnerable

Reading

Part I 🎧 DL 22 💿 CD1-22

Immunization is very important individually and collectively. People who are immunized against a particular disease are very unlikely to catch or develop the disease. Also, if enough members of a particular group are immunized, then any breakouts of the disease will probably be limited.

Without this "herd immunity," diseases can spread out of control. Outbreaks of diseases are disruptive and dangerous to vulnerable members of society, such as children and the elderly.

Everyone in a community is connected to everyone else. People in your circle of friends have different friends who are connected to different friends, and so on. It is often said that almost everyone in the global community is connected to each other by, at most, six people—known as the "six degrees of separation" theory. Of course, identifying which five people might connect you to a villager in Eastern Europe or a city dweller in New Zealand may be difficult, but it is generally possible. In a smaller community, such as a town or city, the connections are easier to trace.

Many diseases that once sickened or killed many people, such as whooping cough, are under control, mostly due to immunizations and better hygiene. Unfortunately, an increasing number of parents are refusing to have their children vaccinated. As a result, fewer members of the community are protected from disease.

Part II 🎧 DL 23 💿 CD1-23

Once the immunization rate of a given population drops below 70%, the chances of an outbreak spreading

Notes

immunization
予防接種

individually and collectively
個人でも集団でも

breakouts
(伝染病、戦争などの)発生

herd immunity
集団免疫

disruptive　破壊的な

the elderly　高齢者

dweller　住民

whooping cough
百日ぜき

hygiene　衛生状態

have ~ vaccinated
~にワクチン接種させる

chances　可能性

out of control are much higher. Sick children will come into contact with a greater number of children who are not immunized, and the disease will spread quickly.

Since it is clearly dangerous for a community to have many unprotected members, why do some parents resist vaccinations? Parents sometimes hear vaccinations are dangerous, so they choose not to have their children immunized.

While vaccines can have side effects that can be severe, the risk that an unprotected child will get sick in a large outbreak is much higher than the risk of getting sick from side effects.

Although social media shows how interconnected we are, it also allows misinformation to spread very quickly. Many parents base their beliefs on unreliable information, and have lost trust in modern medicine.

Thus, doctors and governmental organizations need to find ways to restore that trust, and must educate the public about the benefits and risks of immunization. As more people get immunized, the probability of living a long healthy life will improve.

(407 words)

have ~ immunized
～に（ワクチン接種をして）免疫力を付けさせる

While ~ ～ではあるが

base their beliefs on ~
自分たちの信念の根拠を～に置く

modern medicine
現代医学

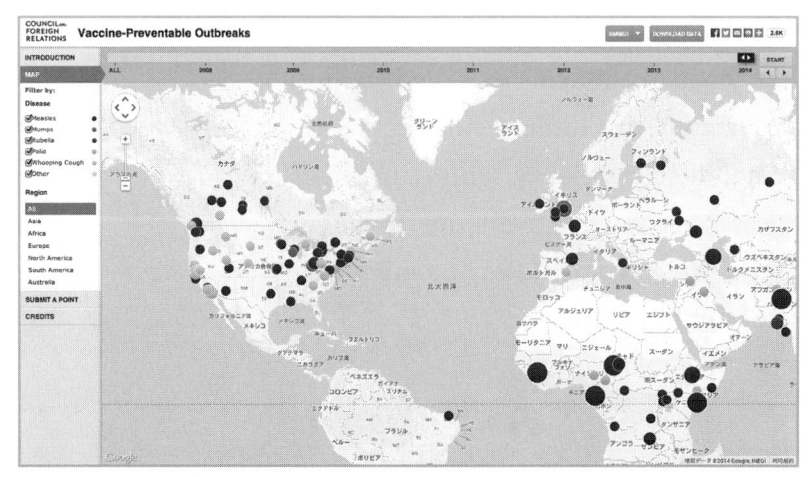

▶ ワクチンの予防接種をすれば防げる病気のことをVPD（vaccine-preventable diseases）といい、これを認知させて予防接種の必要性を普及させようという動きは世界に広がっている。上はVPDの集団発生地域を地図化したVaccine-Preventable Outbreaksというウェブサイト。
www.cfr.org/interactives/GH_Vaccine_Map/index.html#intro

Exercises

Focus on Phrases

語群から（　）に適切な語を入れて英文を完成させましょう。
その際、必要に応じて語形は変えること。

1. The policy is (　　　　) on the fact that the Earth's resources are finite.
2. All the PCs in our office should be (　　　　) from computer viruses.
3. She is not a smoker, but she (　　　　) lung disease last year.
4. My children like cookies, chocolates and cakes, not to (　　　　) ice cream.
5. You will (　　　　) into contact with African culture through this folk music concert.

> come　base　develop　mention　protect

Focus on Contents

本文の内容に合うように（　）に適切な語句を選びましょう。

Part I

1. "Herd immunity" in a society will help (　) the risk of breakouts of disease.
   a. face　**b.** reduce　**c.** underestimate
2. Nowadays the number of unvaccinated children is (　).
   a. refusing　**b.** doubled　**c.** increasing

Part II

1. Some parents don't understand that the risk of side effects is (　) than that of developing a disease.
   a. more severe　**b.** lower　**c.** more unreliable
2. An increased rate of (　) will lead to improved quality of life.
   a. immunization　**b.** misinformation　**c.** modern medicine

Summary

( )にa～eから適切な語を選び、それぞれのPartの要約文を作りましょう。

Part I

Thanks to immunization policies, many fatal diseases that killed people in the past are now under (1.). As illustrated by the so-called "six degrees of separation" theory, people around the world are (2.) to one another very closely. As a result, without "herd immunity," any (3.) of a disease could spread very fast and be (4.) for a large community.

   a. connected   **b.** control   **c.** disruptive   **d.** limited   **e.** outbreak

Part II

The problem is that more and more parents are avoiding vaccinations as they believe (1.) effects might be harmful to their children. However, if a disease broke out, it would spread uncontrollably among (2.) children, posing a threat to the whole community. Parents are requested not to act on (3.) information from social (4.), but voluntarily have their children vaccinated against diseases.

   a. media   **b.** side   **c.** trust   **d.** unprotected   **e.** unreliable

Writing Practice

日本文の意味に合った英文になるように、[ ]内の語句を並べかえましょう。

1. もし免疫を持っていないならば、病気の広がりは手に負えなくなり、社会全体を崩壊させかねない。

   If people are not immunized, the disease can [and / control / disrupt / of / out / spread] the whole community.

2. 我々は、一般の人々が予防接種の効用を信じるように啓発する必要がある。

   We need to [educate / in / the public / put / to / trust] the benefits of vaccination.

40

Geothermal Energy
安定した電力源としての可能性

Unit 7

東日本大震災以来、災害時の安定した電力供給源確保の大切さが再認識されています。こういった社会の動きを受けて注目されているのが地熱発電です。震災後、わずか数日のうちに復旧し、電力供給に貢献したことは広く知られています。化石燃料エネルギーに代わるエネルギーとして以前から名前のあがっているこの発電方式の歴史は長く、すでに100年以上が経過しています。この間、より優れた発電を目指してさまざまな改良が加えられています。

Pre-Exercises

Focus on Words

日本語の意味に合うようにa～f、g～lの各語群から適切な語を選びましょう。

1. 表面にニスを塗る　　　　　apply varnish to the (　　)
2. 蒸気を出す　　　　　　　　spew out (　　)
3. 火山観測所を訪ねる　　　　visit a (　　) observatory
4. 試験管から液体を除去する　clear (　　) from the test tube
5. 筋肉に圧力をかける　　　　apply (　　) on the muscle

　　　a. fluid　　b. generation　　c. pressure
　　　d. surface　　e. vapor　　f. volcano

6. カナダで丸一年過ごす　　　spend an (　　) year in Canada
7. 十分な食料を用意する　　　prepare (　　) amount of foods
8. 大規模な研究を行う　　　　conduct an (　　) research
9. 二次的な問題を起こす　　　cause (　　) problems
10. 通常の生活に戻る　　　　 return to a (　　) life

　　　g. adjacent　　h. entire　　i. extensive
　　　j. normal　　k. secondary　　l. sufficient

Reading

Part I DL 26 CD1-26

Geothermal energy is produced by using natural heat from the Earth's crust. Sometimes this type of heat comes to the surface in the form of a volcano, a geyser, or a hot spring. Heat that would otherwise be trapped in hot rocks or underground reservoirs can be used to generate electricity. Someday the entire planet will rely on geothermal heat for its energy needs, just as Iceland does today.

The first geothermal plant was constructed in Italy in 1904 by Prince Piero Ginori Conti. His system used "dry steam." In this design, naturally escaping steam turns turbines in an electricity generator. Thus, instead of burning coal, oil, or gas to boil water and create turbine-powering steam, these plants simply harness naturally occurring vapor.

Although dry steam plants have a simple design, they require a constant source of steam at a sufficient pressure. Only two places in the world have such reservoirs of dry steam: Larderello, where Conti pioneered geothermal electricity generation, and The Geysers, a field in California that also has an extensive geothermal plant.

Part II DL 27 CD1-27

The next generation of geothermal plants, known as "flash steam," uses two wells. The production well brings up very hot, highly-pressurized water from a geothermal reservoir. The water flows into a tank, quickly loses pressure, and "flashes," or partially turns to steam. The steam is used to turn turbines, and the excess water and condensed steam are returned to the reservoir via the

---

Notes

Geothermal energy
地熱エネルギー

geyser 間欠泉

otherwise be trapped in ~
さもないと~に取り込まれてしまう

hot rocks 高温岩体
underground reservoirs
地下貯水槽

Prince Piero Ginori Conti
プリンス・ピエロ・ジノリ・コンティ (1865-1939)。イタリアのビジネスマンであり政治家

harness 利用する

vapor 蒸気

Larderello
ラルデレロ (イタリア中部トスカーナ州に位置する地熱発電所が集中した地域)

The Geysers
ガイザーズ (カリフォルニア州にある世界最大規模の地熱地帯)

production well
生産井

geothermal reservoir
地熱貯留層 (マグマによって熱せられた高温・高圧の地下水が貯まっている層)

injection well. Most geothermal plants use this design, which was invented in New Zealand.

Third generation plants are known as "binary" plants, as they have two parts. Instead of flashing water from a reservoir, these plants circulate the reservoir water in pipes that loop back into the reservoir.

On the surface, the hot water pipes boil a secondary fluid in adjacent pipes in a heat exchanger. The secondary fluid has a boiling point below 100 ℃, so more of the geothermal heat can be used to produce steam than with the former types of plants.

When the March 11, 2011 earthquake hit northern Japan, one of the nine geothermal plants in the area was offline for maintenance. Six others automatically went offline due to the earthquake. Two continued operating normally, as the earthquake was not so strong where they were located. On March 15, all six of the units that went offline were back in operation, producing the usual amount of electricity.

(400 words)

injection well 注入井

loop back into ~
一巡して～に戻る
secondary fluid
二次流体
adjacent 隣りの
heat exchanger
熱交換器

offline 稼働停止状態

■日本の地熱発電所

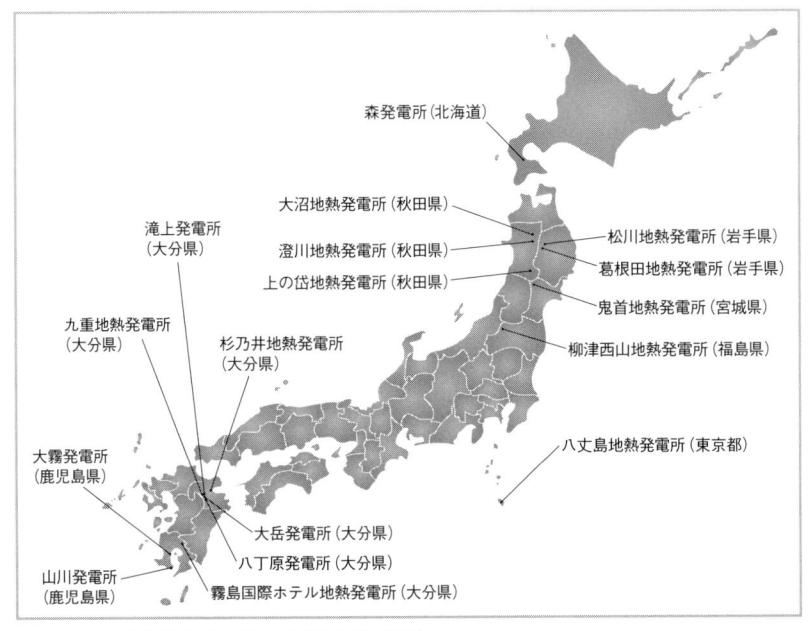

▶ 日本にある地熱発電所は17ヵ所（2014年現在）。

Exercises

Focus on Phrases

語群から（　）に適切な語を入れて英文を完成させましょう。
その際、必要に応じて語形は変えること。

1. Nobody noticed that the generator (　　　　　) offline by accident.
2. After a long discussion, we finally (　　　　　) to a conclusion last week.
3. Last night we got (　　　　　) in heavy traffic.
4. He (　　　　　) up an interesting topic, and we had a nice chat.
5. The factory admitted that some chemicals (　　　　　) into the river.

bring　come　flow　go　trap

Focus on Contents

本文の内容に合うように（　）に適切な語句を選びましょう。

Part I

1. People can make use of the heat from (　) to produce geothermal energy.
   a. coal　**b.** Iceland　**c.** volcanoes
2. For the types of plants invented by Conti, (　) are essential.
   a. coal and oil　**b.** hot springs and vapor　**c.** steam and pressure

Part II

1. The (　) generation of geothermal plants returns excess water to the reservoir.
   a. second　**b.** third　**c.** second and third
2. (　) of the six plants that stopped automatically during the 3.11 earthquake were back to normal within a week.
   a. All　**b.** Half　**c.** None

Summary

（　）にa～eから適切な語を選び、それぞれのPartの要約文を作りましょう。

Part I

The heat of the Earth is usually (1.　) deep underground, but sometimes spouts to the (2.　) of the Earth's crust. It can take the form of a volcanic eruption, or hot water from a hot spring, for example. We can harness this energy in geothermal plants, let the steam turn the (3.　) and generate electricity. The problem is such plants require a constant (4.　) of high-pressure steam.

a. source　**b.** plant　**c.** surface　**d.** turbine　**e.** trapped

Part II

Following the (1.　) steam plants that were developed in the early 20th Century, (2.　) steam systems as well as (3.　) plants were developed. The former brings hot water up to the surface where it is turned to steam in a flash. The latter exchanges heat between two different fluids. The fluids in the pipe on the surface have a (4.　) boiling point, making the system more efficient.

a. lower　**b.** binary　**c.** flash　**d.** dry　**e.** excess

Writing Practice

日本文の意味に合った英文になるように、[　]内の語句を並べかえましょう。

1. 地熱発電所は、化石燃料を燃やすのではなく、自然界に存在する蒸気を利用する。
   Geothermal plants [harness / instead / occurring / of / naturally / vapor] burning fossil fuels.

2. バイナリー発電所と呼ばれる第3世代のシステムは、従来のモデルよりも多くの地熱を利用できる。
   The third generation system, called "binary" plants, can use
   [the geothermal / heat / more of / previous / than] models.

Unit 8 Insects for Food
豊富で栄養価の高い身近な食材

深刻な食糧難が迫っている21世紀。抜群の栄養価を誇り、スピーディーな生産サイクルと格安の飼育コストが保障されている、そんな魅力あふれる食材が実は身近にあるという話を耳にしたことがありませんか。「昆虫食」の話です。この言葉を聞いただけで拒否反応を示す人がいる反面、何の抵抗もなく昆虫を常食としている人がいるのも事実です。稀にみるヘルシーフードであり、量産可能なこの食材の価値は、じゅうぶん再考に値すると考えられます。

Pre-Exercises

Focus on Words

日本語の意味に合うようにa〜f、g〜lの各語群から適切な語を選びましょう。

1. タンパク質をエネルギーに変える   convert (　　) into energy
2. 5グラムの繊維を含む   contain 5 grams of (　　)
3. 大雑把な見積もりを出す   provide a rough (　　)
4. 庭に肥料をまく   spread (　　) in the garden
5. 穀物を製粉する   grind (　　) into flour

a. estimate **b.** fertilizer **c.** fiber
d. grain **e.** pollution **f.** protein

6. 栄養価の高いものを食べる   eat (　　) foods
7. 産業廃棄物の量を減らす   reduce the amount of (　　) waste
8. 有能な秘書を雇う   employ an (　　) secretary
9. 心地よい時間を過ごす   have a (　　) time
10. 持続可能なエネルギー源を見つける find a (　　) energy source

g. comfortable **h.** efficient **i.** healthier
j. industrial **k.** nutritious **l.** sustainable

Reading

Part I

Would you consider having a high-protein burger that came from crickets, not cows? Eating bugs is good for the planet and good for your health. However, before we can get beetle burgers on menus, people will have to accept the idea of eating insects.

Eating bugs is no problem for the billions of people around the world who do so every day. Their ancestors found that insects were a nutritious and delicious, and readily available, source of food.

Scientists assure us that bugs are packed with protein, vitamins, minerals, and fiber, and have much less fat than beef. Because this low-calorie food source doesn't require many resources to grow, the cost of production is low when compared to other sources of protein.

Moreover, instead of producing pollution, as industrial feedlots unfortunately do, insect farms make fertilizer, which helps grow food for the next generation of insects.

Let's take a closer look at beef production. Cows are usually three years old at the time they are slaughtered. They consume a lot of food as they grow. A common estimate is that it takes eight kilograms of feed to produce one kilogram of beef. Corn and other crops that are grown to make this cow feed require the use of a lot of water, pesticides, and energy, in addition to a large area of land.

Part II

On the other hand, mealworms, which are beetle larvae, can be harvested 20 days after they hatch. Only two kilograms of feed is required for each kilogram of mealworms. Also, since they do not require a lot of space,

Notes

crickets コオロギ
bugs 昆虫

readily 手軽に
assure （人に）～だと請け合う
packed with ～ ～がぎっしり詰まっている

pollution 汚染
feedlots 肥育場（市場向けに家畜を囲い込んで太らせる場所）
fertilizer 肥料
are slaughtered 食肉処理される

estimate 見積もり

mealworms ゴミムシダマシ
can be harvested 採取され得る
hatch 卵からかえる

they don't put a burden on the environment.

Another point to consider is that efforts to make beef production more efficient aren't likely to make the beef healthier, or the process more comfortable for the cows.

For example, reducing the space used by cows increases their stress. Also, it seems that giving cattle growth hormones so that they fatten up faster does not make the meat more delicious or healthier.

If we were to start eating lower on the food chain, then we could depend on insects for much of our protein, and, moreover, eat the grains we currently grow for cows. As the world's population increases, we will need to find a sustainable way to feed everyone. The lowly insect may just lead us to a better future.

(391 words)

growth hormones
成長ホルモン

food chain 食物連鎖

sustainable way
持続可能な方法

■世界で食される昆虫の種類と割合

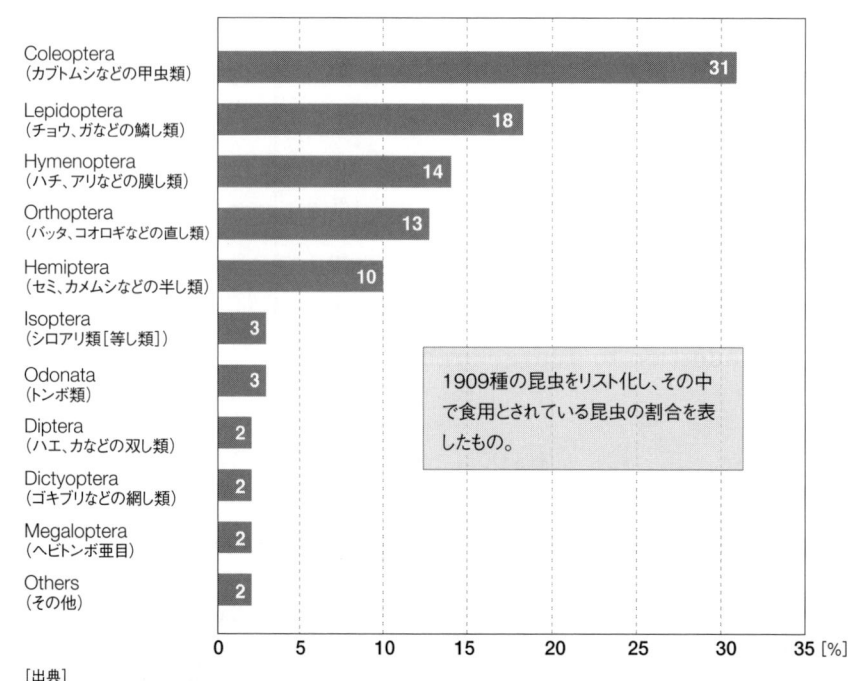

種類	割合 (%)
Coleoptera (カブトムシなどの甲虫類)	31
Lepidoptera (チョウ、ガなどの鱗し類)	18
Hymenoptera (ハチ、アリなどの膜し類)	14
Orthoptera (バッタ、コオロギなどの直し類)	13
Hemiptera (セミ、カメムシなどの半し類)	10
Isoptera (シロアリ類[等し類])	3
Odonata (トンボ類)	3
Diptera (ハエ、カなどの双し類)	2
Dictyoptera (ゴキブリなどの網し類)	2
Megaloptera (ヘビトンボ亜目)	2
Others (その他)	2

1909種の昆虫をリスト化し、その中で食用とされている昆虫の割合を表したもの。

[出典]
FAO, 2013, Edible insects: Future prospects for food and food security p.10, Figure 2.2 "Number of insect species, by order, consumed worldwide"

Exercises

Focus on Phrases

語群から（　）に適切な語を入れて英文を完成させましょう。
その際、必要に応じて語形は変えること。

1. The discovery will ( ) to a breakthrough in the field of biology.
2. He said that our success ( ) out of our teamwork.
3. This book is ( ) with useful advice on healthy living.
4. ( ) to his idea, my idea is boring.
5. I tried to ( ) up my skinny cat.

come　compare　fatten　lead　pack

Focus on Contents

本文の内容に合うように（　）に適切な語句を選びましょう。

Part I

1. ( ) found that insects were nutritious.
   a. Ancestors   b. Travellers   c. Tribes
2. According to scientists, bugs are rich in ( ).
   a. fat   b. carbohydrate   c. protein

Part II

1. Compared to beef, growing beetle larvae is ( ).
   a. environmentally-friendly   b. less cost-effective   c. time-consuming
2. Eating insects is a ( ) way to feed more people.
   a. sustainable   b. common   c. required

Summary

（ ）にa～eから適切な語を選び、それぞれのPartの要約文を作りましょう。

Part I

Though you may not feel like doing it, billions of people around the world eat bugs as part of their ordinary diet. (1.) with protein, vitamins, minerals, etc., they are very (2.). From an economical point of view, they are cost-effective when compared with other sources of protein, such as beef, because they (3.) less feed. Why not (4.) the idea of eating insects?

a. accept **b.** addition **c.** consume **d.** nutritious **e.** packed

Part II

Let's have a closer look at raising cows. Apart from needing large amounts of food, they also (1.) a lot of space, which puts a substantial burden on the environment. On the other hand, if we (2.) this space, it would increase the stress that cows feel. Together with the use of growth hormones, it (3.) to unhealthy meat. If we start eating insects, it would help (4.) the growing population.

a. feed **b.** harvest **c.** leads **d.** reduce **e.** require

Writing Practice

日本文の意味に合った英文になるように、[　]内の語句を並べかえましょう。

1. 昆虫は、容易に入手可能な、低カロリーの食料源となり得るだろう。

   The insects could be [a / available / food / low-calorie / readily / source].

2. 食物連鎖の低い部分を食べるならば、おおいに穀類の節約にもなるだろう。

   If we were to [chain / eat / food / lower / on / the], we could save a great deal of grain, too.

Unit 9

Ivory
象牙取引の現実

ブローチなどの装飾品からハンコのような実用品まで、象牙は身近にある素材のひとつです。象牙製品が多く出回るということはそれだけ多数の象が犠牲になっているということに想像が及ぶ人は多いとは言えません。象の絶滅さえ危惧されることに加えて、象牙取引にかかわる膨大な金銭が、主としてアフリカ諸国を襲っている理不尽な内乱を資金面で助長しているという政治的な問題も絡んでいます。美しい象牙は心を奪うものですが、象牙によって奪われる命があるのが現実です。

Pre-Exercises

Focus on Words

日本語の意味に合うようにa～f、g～lの各語群から適切な語を選びましょう。

1. 全面禁煙 — total (　　) on smoking
2. 外国企業に資本を輸出する — export (　　) to foreign firms
3. 働く気を起こさせる — increase the (　　) to work
4. 感情的打撃を受ける — get an emotional (　　)
5. 愚かな虐殺を避ける — avoid senseless (　　)

a. slaughter　**b.** blow　**c.** capital
d. denture　**e.** incentive　**f.** ban

6. 貴重な版の書籍を収集する — collect (　　) editions of books
7. 実験段階のままに留まる — remain at an (　　) stage
8. 違法な物質を持つ — have an (　　) substance
9. 平和的な外交政策を望む — hope for a (　　) foreign policy
10. 致命傷のリスクを減らす — reduce the risk of a (　　) injury

g. endangered　**h.** experimental　**i.** fatal
j. illegal　**k.** prized　**l.** peaceful

Reading

Part I

Ivory was once a most prized material. Expert pianists were said to "tickle the ivories," meaning that they had an expert, light touch on the piano keyboard. The best personal stamps (*hanko*) and dentures were made of ivory. However, the material's beautiful appearance is now clouded by the knowledge that demand for ivory is driving elephants to extinction.

Not so long ago things looked better for the African elephant. When it became clear that they would disappear from the Earth unless something was done, a worldwide ban on ivory trade was instituted in 1989. Elephant populations, which had been cut in half in the 1980s, began to stabilize or recover.

Demand for ivory did not really let up, and so two experimental sales of ivory took place, in 1997 and 2008. The theory was that the sale of the ivory would give African countries much-needed capital to fund their conservation efforts, and that the increased supply of ivory would lead to lower prices.

However, the effect was quite the opposite of what was intended. First, the sales made it seem that there was no longer a ban on ivory trade. As a result, demand for ivory products went up strongly. At the same time, the ivory seems to have been bought up by a small number of dealers, who have released it on the market little by little. The final result: prices have zoomed up, and poachers now have a very strong incentive to harvest tusks and feed the illegal trade in ivory.

Notes

tickle the ivories
=play the piano
tickleはtouch lightlyという意味。Ivoriesはピアノの白鍵のこと

denture 義歯

is ~ clouded
曇る、陰る

driving ~ to extinction
～を絶滅に追い込んでいる

ban on ~ ～の禁止

was instituted
実施された

let up 止む、弱まる

The theory was that ~
～という目論見だった

conservation efforts
(象の)保護運動

have zoomed up
増大した

incentive 動機

feed ~
～に材料を供給する

Part II

The process is not pretty. Poachers capture an elephant, saw off its tusks, and leave it to die. Smugglers bribe officials and take the ivory out of the country. In destination countries, organized crime gangs sell ivory on the black market. The customers who buy ivory trinkets may not know that they are supporting all this activity, but that is the reality.

African savannahs are no longer peaceful habitats for elephants. Profits from the sale of these tusks go to fund the purchase of weapons used in civil wars and anti-government protests. These weapons end up killing many innocent people, shedding more blood. Consuming ivory supports this bloody ivory trade and allows it to continue to thrive.

As a response to the 1989 ban, Japanese piano makers decided to stop using ivory in their premier pianos. They had long ago stopped using ivory in regular pianos because of the cost. Years of research have since paid off with new materials for piano keys that have all the advantages of ivory but do not depend on the slaughter of endangered animals. However, we need to stop all sales of ivory to avoid a final, fatal blow to elephant populations. (451 words)

Smugglers 密輸業者

organized crime gangs
組織犯罪グループ

go to ~
後ろに不定詞が来る場合は、〜するのに「役立つ」という意味

thrive 盛んになる

premier 最高級の

paid off
=been successful

▶ ジャングルにキャンプを張りながら活動する密猟団に対し、アフリカ諸国は監視の目を強化するも追いついていないのが現状。

Exercises

Focus on Phrases

語群から（　）に適切な語を入れて英文を完成させましょう。
その際、必要に応じて語形は変えること。

1. She promised not to (　　　　　) her mother to despair again.
2. The first book fair will (　　　　　) place in our town next year.
3. Before the typhoon season, I have to (　　　　　) some branches off.
4. Our discussion will (　　　　　) up in failure.
5. All the work has (　　　　　) off.

drive　end　pay　saw　take

Focus on Contents

本文の内容に合うように（　）に適切な語句を選びましょう。

Part I

1. Even after the (　) ban of the ivory trade, the demand for ivory still increased.
   a. local　**b.** international　**c.** illegal
2. Because of the way the ivory was traded, the price of ivory became (　).
   a. higher　**b.** lower　**c.** fixed

Part II

1. Purchasing ivory brings with it a danger of (　) civil wars.
   a. losing　**b.** stopping　**c.** escalating
2. Japanese piano makers contributed to the protection of elephants by (　).
   a. making a law　**b.** creating new piano keys
   c. stopping making premier pianos

Ivory Unit 9

Summary

( )にa〜eから適切な語を選び、それぞれのPartの要約文を作りましょう。

Part I

Ivory has been prized as a material of piano keyboards and others, but the trade is threatening the elephant population. To save African elephants from extinction, a ban on ivory trade was (1.) in 1989. However, demand for ivory was still strong and the regulation was loosened a little. The final result: a limited number of dealers started to control the market and made big profits. The prices that (2.) up were a stronger incentive to (3.) more tusks, a far cry from (4.) the elephants.

a. protecting   b. harvest   c. instituted   d. stabilize   e. zoomed

Part II

The process of ivory smuggling is dirty and cruel. Poachers, smugglers, (1.) officials and organized crime gangs all join in the wrongdoing. If you buy ivory trinkets you would unconsciously help fund the purchase of weapons and in the end help to (2.) more blood. You should not allow such a bloody business to continue to (3.). Recently, piano makers have started to substitute some artificial materials instead of depending on ivory from (4.) animals.

a. bribed   b. capture   c. endangered   d. shed   e. thrive

Writing Practice

日本文の意味に合った英文になるように、[ ]内の語句を並べかえましょう。

1. 象牙の需要の高まりは、期待とは正反対の結果をもたらした。
An increased demand for ivory [expected / led / of / quite the opposite / to / was / what].

2. 象牙の違法取引は、結局は、武器を調達する資金となりかねない。
Illegal ivory trades can [end / funding / of / the purchase / up / weapons].

Unit 10 Maglev Train
疾走する未来のトレイン

実物を見たことがなくても、子供時代からリニアモーターカーの名前を知っていたという人は珍しくありません。空気抵抗を極限まで減らすために長く尖った先端部分を持つ流線型の車体、レールから浮き上がり、摩擦から完全に解き放たれて疾走する姿、時速500キロを上回るスピードが出せる性能―リニアモーターカーには憧れを刺激する要素がいくつもあります。2013年に山梨県で行われた大規模な試験走行の成功は、憧れを現実に大きく近づけました。

Pre-Exercises

Focus on Words

日本語の意味に合うようにa～f、g～lの各語群から適切な語を選びましょう。

1. 物理を専攻する　　　　　　　　　major in (　　)
2. 公共の交通機関を利用する　　　　take public (　　)
3. その金属の特質を分析する　　　　analyze the (　　) of the metal
4. 海流にさらわれる　　　　　　　　get washed away by the ocean (　　)
5. 特許を侵害する　　　　　　　　　violate a (　　)

a. current　**b.** patent　**c.** physics
d. pole　**e.** properties　**f.** transportation

6. 根本的な原因を突き止める　　　　find out the (　　) cause
7. 特定の条件を満たす　　　　　　　meet (　　) conditions
8. 反対の見方をする　　　　　　　　take the (　　) view
9. 背後にある複雑な事情を知る　　　know (　　) circumstances behind it
10. ショーで実物大のロボットを展示する　display a (　　) robot in a show

g. certain　**h.** commercial　**i.** complicated
j. fundamental　**k.** full-sized　**l.** opposite

Reading

Part I

The word "maglev" might be new to many people, however, before too long it will likely be a household name. The word maglev comes from the words magnetic (mag) and levitation (lev), giving us the meaning "to raise and levitate something by electromagnetic force," which describes the fundamental physics behind this new technology of train transportation.

A magnet is a special metal with the power to either pull certain metals, for example iron or steel, toward it or push them away. That is, magnets have the power to either attract or repel, and this power is called magnetism. In addition, every magnet has a north and south pole. Similar poles of two magnets will repel each other and opposite poles of two magnets will attract each other.

Electromagnetism is a magnetic force that is generated by electricity. Electromagnets only have power when electricity is passed through them. When the electricity is turned off, the magnetic force is lost.

Furthermore, the poles of an electromagnet are related to the direction of the electric current. If the direction of the electric current is reversed, the poles of the magnet will also be reversed. Maglev trains are thus pulled and pushed forward by this property of electromagnetism.

The system that powers the maglev trains is both quite simple and complicated. Magnets are placed on the tracks and also on the train itself. The magnets are positioned to repel each other, which pushes the train up off the track into a floating position, approximately 15 millimeters above the track. The train moves forward because the electromagnets, which are controlled by alternating electric currents, push and pull the train forward.

Notes

household
=very well known

levitation
空中への浮揚 (動詞形は次行のlevitate)

electromagnetic force
電磁気の力

iron or steel
鉄や鋼 (鋼は、鉄に炭素その他の元素が添加された合金)

a north and south pole
磁極のN極とS極 (地球の場合は北極の近くにS極が、南極の近くにN極がある)

property 特性、特質

tracks (列車の)軌道

Part II

Although the maglev uses cutting-edge technology, the idea has been around for a long time. German scientist Alfred Zehden was awarded a patent for an electromagnetic train back in 1907, more than 100 years ago. In the late 1940's a British electrical engineer developed the first full-sized working model of a train powered by electromagnetism.

The first commercial maglev train was introduced in the U.K. in 1984 at Birmingham International Airport. However, it closed after 11 years as the system was not very reliable.

Currently the most famous maglev train is the one being developed by the Central Japan Railway Company. This work started in 1969, and by 1979 it achieved a speed of 517 km/h, a world record at the time.

In 2003 a speed of 581 km/h was achieved. If all goes according to plan, a high-speed maglev train service will begin operating between Nagoya and Tokyo in 2027.

(426 words)

cutting-edge 最先端の
has been around 存在しており、利用可能だった

full-sized 実物大の
working 実用の

Currently 今日、現在
Central Japan Railway Company JR東海。略称はJR Central
at the time その当時（at that timeでも同じ）

▶ 2013年に行われた、リニア中央新幹線試験走行の車内。2027年に開業予定の新幹線は最高時速505キロで東京・名古屋間を約40分で移動する。

Exercises

Focus on Phrases

語群から（　）に適切な語を入れて英文を完成させましょう。
その際、必要に応じて語形は変えること。

1. In my school days, my inspirations always (　　　　) from chats with friends.
2. Some students saw a suspicious person (　　　　) through the corridor.
3. Could you (　　　　) off the radio, please? I can't hear you.
4. Sometimes a lack of appetite is (　　　　) to a lack of sleep.
5. The shop clerk took a red coat from a shelf and (　　　　) it on a hanger.

come   turn   pass   place   relate

Focus on Contents

本文の内容に合うように（　）に適切な語句を選びましょう。

Part I

1. Magnetism is the power of a magnet functioning in (　) direction.
   a. a multiple   b. either the opposite or the same   c. an unpredictable
2. In order to float maglev trains off the track, magnets are located to produce (　).
   a. a repelling power   b. alternating electric currents
   c. the power of north and south poles

Part II

1. The idea of maglev trains dates back to (　) century.
   a. the early 20th   b. the middle of 20th   c. the end of 19th
2. The first commercial maglev train in the U.K. was not successful because the system was (　).
   a. full-sized   b. infamous   c. unreliable

Summary

（　）にa～eから適切な語を選び、それぞれのPartの要約文を作りましょう。

Part I

Everybody is familiar with the working of magnets: how they attract or repel each other. Now you can generate strong magnetic power by electricity—called electromagnetism—and use it as a (1.　) force of trains. The system is rather complicated. First, the (2.　) power levitates the train into a (3.　) position above the track. Secondly, both the pulling and pushing magnetic powers—which are controlled by an (4.　) electric current—move the train forward.

a. alternating　**b.** driving　**c.** floating　**d.** passing　**e.** repelling

Part II

To be sure, magnetic trains are at the (1.　) edge of modern technology. It was as early as 1907 that the basic idea of a maglev train was put into practice by German scientist Alfred Zehden. Since then, full-sized working models have been introduced in some countries. Currently, the leading type of maglev train has been developed in Japan, (2.　) a speed of 581 km/h in 2003. (3.　) to plans, new maglev trains will be (4.　) commercially in 2027.

a. according　**b.** achieving　**c.** cutting　**d.** including　**e.** operating

Writing Practice

日本文の意味に合った英文になるように、[　]内の語句を並べかえましょう。

1. 人々にとって、この物理的特性の基本が、やがてなじみのものとなることだろう。
   People will become [before / familiar / fundamental / long / physics / the / with].

2. マグレヴのアイデアは、チェーデンが特許を取った1907年以降、世に知られている。
   The maglev [around / been / has / idea / since 1907 / when] Zehden got the patent for it.

Robots
活躍の場を広げるロボット

Unit 11

近年、猛烈な寒波に襲われる地域が増えました。記録的降雪により集落が孤立するニュースはもはや珍しくはありません。自然に対する人間の無力さを思い知らされるようなこういった災害時に威力を発揮するのがレスキューロボットです。除雪や瓦礫の撤去を主な仕事とするロボットと、被災者の捜索・救助が中心のロボットの双方で開発が進んでおり、活躍の場を異にする癒し系ロボットと共に、ロボット産業の未来を担う新鋭機として期待が寄せられています。

Pre-Exercises

Focus on Words

日本語の意味に合うようにa〜f、g〜lの各語群から適切な語を選びましょう。

1. 経済の崩壊に直面する　　　face an economic (　　)
2. 大規模な雪崩を引き起こす　trigger a large (　　)
3. 険しい崖をのぼる　　　　　climb a steep (　　)
4. 腫瘍摘出手術を受ける　　　undergo (　　) to remove a tumor
5. 夜明けに出発する　　　　　leave at (　　)

> **a.** avalanche　**b.** cliff　**c.** dawn
> **d.** collapse　**e.** surgery　**f.** victim

6. 人為的な気候変動を調査する　investigate (　　) climate change
7. 最大限の支援を与える　　　　give (　　) support
8. 二次感染の危険性　　　　　　the risk of a (　　) infection
9. 離れた場所を探査する　　　　explore a (　　) region
10. 途方もなく大きな影響を与える　have a (　　) effect

> **g.** cool　**h.** man-made　**i.** maximum
> **j.** remote　**k.** secondary　**l.** tremendous

Reading

Part I 🎧 DL 42 💿 CD2-10

Robots, once the stuff of science fiction, are increasingly being used to help with our everyday lives. One robot that has people turning their heads is the T-52 Enryu Rescue Robot from Japan. Even the name Enryu which means rescue dragon in Japanese is cool. The T-52 Enryu is one of the world's largest rescue robots. It was designed to help rescue victims of large natural disasters such as earthquakes, or man-made disasters such as building collapses.

To help out in these disasters, the T-52 needs to be dragon-sized. It is 3.45 meters high, 2.4 meters wide and weighs a whopping five tons. The T-52 has two long arms each about six meters in length and each arm can lift over 500 kilograms. The rescue robot has super-human strength, so it can easily remove heavy objects after an earthquake, making it easier for rescuers to look for and find survivors trapped under rubble and debris.

Unlike a dragon, the T-52 runs on diesel. It has a maximum speed of three km/h and runs on tracks, so it moves around much like a tank or a bulldozer. It can be operated by an operator riding on the robot or remotely if there is a danger of a secondary disaster.

Part II 🎧 DL 43 💿 CD2-11

The T-52 was also tested for use in accidents related to snow. In Japan, accidents related to snow are becoming more common. There have been many people killed in avalanches or from heavy snow falling from roofs. So researchers decided to test out the T-52 in the snow. The rescue dragon was given the task of rescuing victims from

Notes

the stuff 素材

help with ~
~を手伝う

has people turning their heads
人々を振り向かせる

Enryu
援竜（次ページの写真を参照）

help out
（困難な状況下で）手助けする

dragon-sized
=very big

whopping 桁外れの

rubble and debris
瓦礫や残骸（両者はほぼ同じ意味）

runs on diesel
ディーゼル油で駆動する
diesel=diesel fuel
onはon gasoline, on electricityのように「燃料、動力源」を示す前置詞

tank 戦車

avalanches 雪崩

cars buried under the snow after a large avalanche. To simulate avalanche conditions, a car was placed under the snow at the base of a cliff. The T-52 had to find the car, retrieve and move it to a safe place.

In such conditions, rescuers need to worry about secondary disasters, so in this case the remote function was used.

Although rescuers need to move quickly, they also need to stay safe. Moving a car buried deep under the snow requires a tremendous amount of power. In the experiment, the T-52 was able to get the car out of the snow and allowed the rescuers to work from a safe distance away.

In the future, as technology develops, we will likely see many more types of robots. In the not too distant future, we will likely see robots used for surgery in hospitals, or robots that can act as waiters or cooks in busy restaurants. The robot age is just at its dawn.

(431 words)

simulate
模擬実験をする

retrieve 救出する

In the not too distant future
さほど遠くない将来に
surgery 外科手術
at its dawn
始まったばかりである

▶ T-52（61ページの写真）の後継機として、2007年にはT-53援竜が開発された。より軽量・コンパクト化され、動作も精密になった同機は日本を代表する技術としてニコニコ超会議でも展示された。

Exercises

Focus on Phrases

語群から（　）に適切な語を入れて英文を完成させましょう。
その際、必要に応じて語形は変えること。

1. The speed of his talk (　　　　　) it harder for the audience to understand what he said.
2. Soon after getting her license, she started to (　　　　　) for a job as a pharmacist.
3. I enjoyed (　　　　　) on horseback along the mountain path.
4. Unfortunately he was injured after (　　　　　) from a ladder.
5. I was (　　　　　) to take a day off tomorrow.

allow   fall   look   make   ride

Focus on Contents

本文の内容に合うように（　）に適切な語句を選びましょう。

Part I

1. The T-52 is a (　　) robot which can rescue disaster victims.
   a. one-handed   **b.** huge   **c.** German
2. In order to avoid (　　), people can control the T-52 from a distance.
   a. a large avalanche   **b.** rubble and debris   **c.** a secondary disaster

Part II

1. The T-52 (　　) on a snowy site.
   a. is able to work properly   **b.** can't rescue victims
   c. has never tested its performance
2. In future, robots can be used in more places as (　　) for humans.
   a. representatives   **b.** substitutes   **c.** symbols

Robots   Unit 11

Summary

（　）にa～eから適切な語を選び、それぞれのPartの要約文を作りましょう。

Part I

Robot technology is advancing at an amazing speed. One of the latest feats is the T-52 Enryu from Japan. Named after the legendary dragon, the Enryu is a (1.　) robot of huge bulk, running on caterpillar (2.　). The Enryu is able to move around a debris-scattered (3.　) area to help save (4.　). One can operate the robot by remote control, allowing it to tackle jobs that are too dangerous for men.

a. collapse　**b.** disaster　**c.** rescue　**d.** tracks　**e.** victims

Part II

The T-52 can also display great ability when snow-(1.　) disasters occur. An avalanche, for example, can trap and crush a vehicle under a large amount of snow. In an experiment that (2.　) an avalanche, the Enryu successfully (3.　) a car that had been (4.　) deep under the snow and moved it back to a safer place. In the future, you will see various types of new robots even in hospitals or in restaurants.

a. buried　**b.** related　**c.** retrieved　**d.** simulated　**e.** worried

Writing Practice

日本文の意味に合った英文になるように、[　]内の語句を並べかえましょう。

1. そのロボットは、災害時の救助に超人的な力を発揮したが、それが人々の注目を集めた。
   The robot displayed a super-human power to help out in disasters, [had / heads / people / their / turning / which].

2. さまざまなタイプのロボットの登場を待つ今、ロボット時代はまさに始まったばかりである。
   With various types of robots ready to come on the scene, the [at / dawn / is / its / just / robot age].

Unit 12 International Space Station
約400キロ上空の実験施設

明け方や夕方にふと空を見上げた時、明るく輝きながら移動する物体を見かけたことはありませんか。おそらくそれは国際宇宙ステーションです。遥か彼方の宇宙を舞台に幅広い分野の研究、観察を行っているこの有人実験施設は、組み立て作業開始以来、熱い注目を浴びています。実験風景のインターネット配信や実験テーマの一般公募などの試みは、宇宙という特殊環境での先端研究を身近に感じさせるものとして科学者だけでなく一般の人々にも好評です。

Pre-Exercises

Focus on Words

日本語の意味に合うようにa～f、g～lの各語群から適切な語を選びましょう。

1. 人工衛星を宇宙に打ち上げる　　launch a (　　) into space
2. 宇宙船を軌道に乗せる　　send a spacecraft into (　　)
3. 地下水を求めて調査を始める　　begin (　　) for groundwater
4. 地球の重力を感じる　　sense the earth's (　　)
5. 使命を果たす　　carry out a (　　)

a. exploration　**b.** gravity　**c.** mission
d. module　**e.** orbit　**f.** satellite

6. 星空の下で眠る　　sleep under a (　　) sky
7. タオルで裸身を隠す　　hide my (　　) body with a towel
8. 長期に及ぶ関係を確立する　　establish a (　　) relationship
9. 身体機能を調節する　　regulate (　　) function
10. 決定的な証拠を提供する　　provide (　　) evidence

g. bodily　**h.** crucial　**i.** long-term
j. naked　**k.** solar　**l.** starry

Reading

Part I   DL 46 CD2-14

On a dark starry night, look up into the sky and you'll likely see satellites zooming across the night sky. Keep looking and you might see a much larger object crossing the sky. The International Space Station (ISS) goes around the Earth every 92 minutes, and can easily be spotted with the naked eye. It's so large that you might be fooled into thinking that the ISS is a large passenger jet flying high in the sky.

Construction of the space station began in 1998. Modules for it were built on Earth and carried into orbit and assembled in space. It took 136 flights to bring all the modules up into space and 1,920 man-hours to put the modules together and assemble the space station.

The ISS flies at 7.71 kilometers a second. At that speed, it could go to the moon and back in a single day. The solar panels on the ISS are large enough to cover eight basketball courts. It has the same living space as two large jumbo passenger jets. It has two bathrooms and a gymnasium that researchers use to keep fit and maintain their health.

The ISS flies in a low orbit around the Earth. Its orbit is not a perfect circle. Its perigee, or its closest approach to Earth, is around 410 kilometers and its apogee, its farthest approach, is around 425 kilometers above the earth.

Part II   DL 47 CD2-15

The ISS is a microgravity research laboratory. Research is needed to help humankind prepare for a prolonged stay in a spacecraft. It is important for scientists to know how living in space for extended periods of time will affect the

---

Notes

zooming across ~
〜を素早く横切って進んでいる

The International Space Station
国際宇宙ステーション

can easily be spotted with ~
〜で容易に見つけられる

be fooled into ~
だまされて〜する

Modules
モジュール（特定の機能を持った宇宙船の一部を成す構成区画。2014年8月現在、最大規模のモジュールは日本の実験棟「きぼう」）

man-hours
人時（にんじ）。1人1時間当たりの平均仕事量

assemble 組み立てる

cover ~ 〜の広さに及ぶ

gymnasium 体育館

keep fit 元気でいる

low orbit 低軌道

perigee
近地点（月や人工衛星が軌道上でもっとも地球に近づく点）⇔apogee（遠地点）

closest approach
最接近⇔furthest approach

microgravity 微小重力

human body. Scientists on board the ISS study muscle atrophy—the loss of muscle tissue, and how microgravity affects blood and other bodily fluids when they move around the body. They do research into how cells and plants grow in zero gravity. Scientists also study how things can be manufactured in space, for example how metals form in low gravity environments.

　This research is an important step towards further long-term space exploration. By keeping the ISS in orbit, scientists also learn how to keep and maintain a spacecraft in good working order over a period of years. Thanks to the ISS, we are getting crucial knowledge about how to survive in space for longer periods of time, knowledge that is needed for future space research. Currently, NASA is developing a long-range Mars exploration program. These missions will all be built on the knowledge and know-how that we get from research aboard the ISS. (426 words)

Scientists on board the ISS
国際宇宙ステーションに乗船している科学者たち
muscle atrophy
筋萎縮
tissue 組織
bodily fluids 体液
zero gravity 無重力
be manufactured
製造される

in good working order
正常に運航できる状態
over a period of years
長年にわたって
crucial きわめて重要な
NASA
アメリカ航空宇宙局
National Aeronautics and Space Administrationの略
Mars exploration program
火星探査計画

▶ 国際宇宙ステーション（ISS）の船外活動（組み立て作業）の様子。

International Space Station   Unit 12

Exercises

Focus on Phrases

語群から（　）に適切な語を入れて英文を完成させましょう。
その際、必要に応じて語形は変えること。

1. Emily was so surprised and (   ) up into her mother's face.
2. Don't be (   ) into believing that her story is true.
3. (   ) the whole thing together, we concluded that our decision was right.
4. My doctor advised me to get physical exercise so that I could (   ) fit.
5. He took two weeks off with pay and enjoyed the (   ) vacation.

fool　look　keep　extend　put

Focus on Contents

本文の内容に合うように（　）に適切な語句を選びましょう。

Part I

1. (   ) of the construction work for the International Space Station was carried out in space.
   a. All　**b.** None　**c.** Part
2. The International Space Station has facilities which enable researchers to (   ).
   a. go around the Moon every 92 minutes　**b.** watch free movies
   c. lead a healthy life

Part II

1. Researchers in the International Space Station conduct research (   ).
   a. that only looks at physics　**b.** in a variety of fields
   c. ignoring the effects of gravity on the human body
2. The results of research on board are expected to (   ).
   a. contribute to future space missions　**b.** be kept secret forever
   c. be kept exclusively by NASA

Summary

( )にa〜eから適切な語を選び、それぞれのPartの要約文を作りましょう。

Part I

The construction of the International Space Station (ISS) started in 1998. As many as 136 rockets had to be launched in order to carry necessary (1.) up into (2.). Then, the modules were put together to assemble the space station. It took them 1,920 man-hours in total to complete it. Getting energy from big solar (3.), this space complex provides plenty of living space and other comfortable facilities for the researchers to maintain their (4.).

a. approach　**b.** health　**c.** modules　**d.** orbit　**e.** panels

Part II

Someday, humans will venture out on long space voyages and the research on (1.) the ISS will surely contribute to such a long-term project. For example, scientists are studying how blood moves around the body, and how cells grow under the condition of zero (2.). Also they are learning about the maintenance of a spaceship to keep it working in good (3.). They will need to make the most of these studies in the upcoming (4.) to Mars.

a. board　**b.** fluid　**c.** gravity　**d.** mission　**e.** order

Writing Practice

日本文の意味に合った英文になるように、[ ]内の語句を並べかえましょう。

1. ISSは夜空をとても速く飛ぶので、だまされて、それを大型ジェットとみなすかもしれない。
   The ISS flies so fast across the night sky, that we [for / be fooled / into / it / might / taking] a large jet plane.

2. ISS船上での研究から得たノウハウは、我々の宇宙での長期の生存に役立つことだろう。
   The [aboard / from / know-how / research / that / we get] the ISS will contribute to our survival in space for longer periods of time.

Pipe Organ
技術が生み出す多彩な音色

Unit 13

パイプオルガンは、大ホールや教会といった特定の場所にあるにもかかわらず、音色が広く親しまれている楽器です。パイプオルガンとの最初の出会いが、音楽の授業で聴いたバッハの「小フーガト短調」という人も少なくありません。たった一台の楽器とは思えないほどの迫力ある重厚な響きと、ささやき声にも似た繊細な音が自在に出せる理由は、ずらっと並ぶパイプとペダルにあります。そこでは、何世紀も前のテクノロジーを見ることができるのです。

Pre-Exercises

Focus on Words

日本語の意味に合うように a〜f、g〜l の各語群から適切な語を選びましょう。

1. 楽器を手に取って演奏する　　pick up an (　　) and play it
2. 礼拝所を訪ねる　　visit a place of (　　)
3. 古い大聖堂を改修する　　renovate an old (　　)
4. その伝説の起源を調べる　　trace the (　　) of the legend
5. 自然の驚異に興奮する　　become excited about a (　　) of nature

> **a.** cathedral　**b.** instrument　**c.** marvel
> **d.** note　**e.** origin　**f.** worship

6. 強力な薬を処方する　　prescribe (　　) medicine
7. 複数の選択肢を与える　　offer (　　) options
8. 同時通訳をする　　do (　　) interpretation
9. 圧縮カラー画像を送信する　　send (　　) color images
10. やさしく扱う　　treat in a (　　) manner

> **g.** complex　**h.** compressed　**i.** gentle
> **j.** multiple　**k.** simultaneous　**l.** powerful

Reading

Part I

    If you've never heard the powerful sound of a pipe organ reverberating around the stone walls of an old church, it is an experience you won't soon forget. The pipe organ is called the king of instruments and it is truly one of the most amazing musical instruments in the world. Commonly connected with Christian worship in churches and cathedrals, the pipe organ has been part of western culture for hundreds of years. The origins of the pipe organ date back two thousand years to the 3rd Century B.C. in Greece.

    Pipe organs are large and complex. They have pipes for making sounds, a wind system for forcing air into the pipes and keyboards for controlling the sounds that are made. Each pipe produces a single sound and so multiple pipes are needed to create the different musical notes. The pipes are then fitted together in a case that is often the size of an entire room. Sounds are made by forcing air down the pipes.

    High sounds are made by smaller pipes and low sounds are made by larger pipes. The quality and volume of the sound depend on the volume of the air that is blown into the pipe. Each pipe has a stop mechanism for controlling the air that goes into the pipe.

    A wind system is needed to force compressed air into the pipes. In early times, this was done by using a kind of wind pump called a bellows. However, the bellows was hand operated and often needed many people to operate it. As technology developed the hand-operated bellows was replaced by water engines, then steam engines, gasoline engines and eventually electricity.

Notes

reverberating
反響している

date back two thousand years to ~
〜まで2000年さかのぼる

the 3rd Century B.C.
紀元前3世紀（B.C.=before Christの略。西暦［紀元］はA.D.=Anno Domini［ラテン語］）

wind system
送風装置

multiple 多数の

musical notes 楽音

are then fitted together
その後、（整然と）はめ込まれる

is blown into ~
〜に吹き込まれる

compressed air
圧縮空気

In early times 昔は

bellows
ふいご（気密な空間の体積を変化させることで空気の流れを生み出す器具）

Part II

Organs are complex instruments to play. In addition to the keyboards, they also have a system of pedals and stops. The pedals act much like the keyboard, controlling the air that goes into the pipes, and therefore controlling the sound. There are often up to 30 pedals which the organist must operate simultaneously along with the keyboard.

The stops on an organ control the kind of sound that the pipes produce. When the stops are set in different positions, the pipes can sound like different instruments. You can set them to create a gentle sound like a flute or a strong powerful sound like a trumpet. You can also change the quality of the sound. You can set the stops to sound like a reed instrument, such as a clarinet or an oboe, or a stringed instrument, such as a violin.

Walk into a church and listen to the organ and think about the technology that was needed to build it. Think about the work being done around 500 years ago before electricity and modern manufacturing methods were available. Although an instrument, the pipe organ is also a marvel of engineering.

(468 words)

---

keyboards 鍵盤

stops
音栓、ストップ（音管への風の入り口を開け閉めする装置）

simultaneously
同時に

reed instrument
リード楽器（リードとは、葦や竹、金属などで作られた薄い板のことで、吹き口から空気を送ってこれを振動させ、音を出す）

stringed instrument
弦楽器

marvel 驚異

▶ 鍵盤の左右に並ぶのが「ストップ」。パイプとつながっていて、このストップと鍵盤下の「ペダル」を操作することで、さまざまな音色が作り出される。

Exercises

Focus on Phrases

語群から（　）に適切な語を入れて英文を完成させましょう。
その際、必要に応じて語形は変えること。

1. Our facial expressions are often (　　　　) with our feelings.
2. The origin of this ritual (　　　　) back to the Stone Age.
3. In order to get rid of insects, we tried to (　　　　) smoke into their nests.
4. We decided to (　　　　) an old computer with a new one.
5. (　　　　) into the forest, we enjoyed the songs of many birds.

    blow connect date go replace

Focus on Contents

CheckLink

本文の内容に合うように（　）に適切な語句を選びましょう。

Part I

1. To create colorful sounds, pipe organs need (　　) pipes.
   a. long **b.** large **c.** many
2. (　　) has been commonly used to produce a pipe organ sound recently.
   a. Water engine **b.** Electricity **c.** Human power

Part II

1. In terms of controlling the sound, (　　) have similar functions.
   a. stops and pedals **b.** keyboards and stops **c.** pedals and keyboards
2. The technology needed to build pipe organs is (　　) based on modern manufacturing methods.
   a. not **b.** partly **c.** entirely

Pipe Organ Unit 13

Summary

（　）にa〜eから適切な語を選び、それぞれのPartの要約文を作りましょう。

Part I

DL 52　CD2-20

The pipe organ is an (1.　) musical instrument. It originated in Greece more than 2,000 years ago. It has been an important part of (2.　) culture. A pipe organ blows (3.　) air into "pipes" to produce different musical notes, but intriguingly, each pipe makes just a (4.　) pitch of sound, and so, many pipes of various lengths are needed to create different notes. Necessarily, the whole system can be as big as a room.

a. amazing　**b.** traditional　**c.** single　**d.** compressed　**e.** Christian

Part II

DL 53　CD2-21

Organ playing is quite complicated. First, working the keyboard and pedals, the organist chooses the pipes and (1.　) the quantity of air that is blown into it. Added to this, the organist must (2.　) stops, too, in order to (3.　) sound quality. So the player can (4.　) various sounds—gentle, mellow, or powerful tones, for example—as if they were played by an utterly different kind of instrument, like a violin or a trumpet.

a. controls　**b.** change　**c.** manufacture　**d.** operate　**e.** produce

Writing Practice

日本文の意味に合った英文になるように、[　]内の語句を並べかえましょう。

1. のちには、送風システムとして、蒸気エンジンが手動のふいごに取って代わった。
   Later, [as / bellows / engines / hand-operated / replaced / steam] the wind system.

2. 2000年以上も前にオルガンが演奏されていたことを、まあ、ちょっと考えてみてください。
   [about / being / just / played / the organ / think] more than 2,000 years ago.

Unit 14

Earthquake and Detection Systems
命を守るテクノロジー

私たちはいつ、どこで大地震に見舞われるかわかりません。例えば、電車に乗っている時に激しい揺れを感じる可能性は誰もが持っています。東日本大震災の発生時、通常運転していた東北新幹線が地震検知システムの働きによって大惨事を免れた話はよく知られています。以来、このシステムの研究、開発のスピードには加速度がつきました。初期微動をいち早く感知して送電を全面ストップするまでの時間は短縮され続け、0.5秒が目標値となっています。

Pre-Exercises

Focus on Words

日本語の意味に合うようにa〜f、g〜lの各語群から適切な語を選びましょう。

1. 地域に安定をもたらす　　　　　bring stability to a (　　)
2. 意味の深さを理解する　　　　　understand the (　　) of meaning
3. 世代格差を無視する　　　　　　ignore a generation (　　)
4. 計算を間違える　　　　　　　　make a mistake in (　　)
5. あらゆる手段をとる　　　　　　take all (　　)

> **a.** calculation　**b.** depth　**c.** gap
> **d.** measures　**e.** region　**f.** velocity

6. 大金を稼ぐ　　　　　　　　　　earn a (　　) amount of money
7. 破壊的な行為を避ける　　　　　avoid (　　) behavior
8. 第一次情報源を見つけ出す　　　find a (　　) information source
9. 高度な科学技術に頼る　　　　　rely on a highly (　　) technology
10. 参加者の平均年齢を確認する　　check the (　　) age of participants

> **g.** advanced　**h.** average　**i.** emergency
> **j.** destructive　**k.** massive　**l.** primary

Reading

Part I

Japan's famous bullet train, or *Shinkansen*, reaches speeds of up to 275 km/h on its journey from Tokyo up to Morioka in the Tohoku region of Japan. And on March 11, 2011, 33 trains were racing along the tracks when the Tohoku region was struck by a massive earthquake. Yet miraculously, no one was injured.

In point of fact, it wasn't a miracle. It was science that saved the lives of many that day. A short 12 seconds before the earthquake hit the main island of Honshu, a seismometer belonging to JR East, the operator of the *Shinkansen* in the region, picked up the coming earthquake and sent off signals to all 33 trains triggering an emergency brake, bringing the trains to a speedy stop.

The speed of an earthquake is not constant. There are different kinds of waves, highly destructive S-waves and less-destructive but faster moving P-waves. P-waves are the primary waves, and they are the first shocks that you will feel in an earthquake. The S-waves are secondary waves. These are the strong waves that move the ground back and forth during an earthquake.

Although the speeds can vary depending on the depth and the type of rock that the waves must move through, S-waves are slower than P-waves. P-waves travel between 4 and 13 km/sec while S-waves travel between 3.5 and 7.5 km/sec, approximately 50 to 60% of the velocity of P-waves. This difference creates a time gap which allows warnings to go out.

Part II

This P-wave detection system saved many lives on

March 11, however it is not a guarantee that advance notice of an earthquake will always be given. The system works better the further away it is from the epicenter. If the epicenter of the earthquake is near to the detection system, there won't be enough of a time difference to give advance notice.

We can see this by doing some simple calculations. If you are 240 kilometers away from the epicenter, the P-waves will travel at an average speed of 8 km/sec and the S-waves will travel at 60% of that, 4.8 km/sec. At that rate, the P-waves will take 30 seconds to arrive and the S-waves will take 50 seconds to arrive, giving people 20 seconds to prepare. This means that if the detection system is only 24 kilometers away from the epicenter, the time difference will only be a mere 2 seconds.

The advantage of this detection system is unquestionable, but it does have its limitations. High speed train lines should not be built directly over faults or near potential epicenters, as there might not be enough time to take safety measures.

(438 words)

guarantee	保証
epicenter	震央（震源の真上にある地表の場所。ちなみに「震源」は地震が起きた地中の箇所。英語ではfocus）
faults	断層
take safety measures	安全策を講じる

▶ 2011年4月29日、JR仙台駅に到着する東北新幹線はやて。大地震からわずか1ヵ月半後のこの日、東北新幹線は全線が開通した。

Earthquake and Detection Systems   Unit 14

Exercises

Focus on Phrases

語群から（　）に適切な語を入れて英文を完成させましょう。
その際、必要に応じて語形は変えること。

1. Many parts of Australia were (　　　　　) by a heat wave.
2. This machine is so sophisticated that it can (　　　　　) up all the sounds emitted by animals.
3. I used to (　　　　　) to a geoscience club during my high school days.
4. Further discussions finally (　　　　　) us to an agreement of opinion.
5. We can decide what to do next (　　　　　) on the weather report.

> belong   bring   depend   pick   strike

Focus on Contents

本文の内容に合うように（　）に適切な語句を選びましょう。

Part I

1. Thanks to (　　), *Shinkansen* operators could manage to stop their trains before the outbreak of the 3.11 earthquake.
   a. the conductors' judgment
   b. an e-mail from JR East
   c. signals from a seismometer
2. The type of rocks has (　　) impact on the difference in speed between S-waves and P-waves.
   a. some   b. no   c. little

Part II

1. The (　　) decides how many seconds in advance we can get the warning.
   a. place of the detection system   b. earthquake size   c. operators' ability
2. For our safety, it is essential to check the place of (　　) before building high speed train lines.
   a. faults and possible epicenters   b. detection systems   c. train stations

Summary

（　）にa〜eから適切な語を選び、それぞれのPartの要約文を作りましょう。

Part I   DL 56   CD2-24

On March 11th, 2011, the Tohoku Region was hard hit by a (1.　) earthquake, and, at that time, 33 *Shinkansen* trains were traveling in the area. Fortunately, however, not a single passenger was injured, thanks to the (2.　) warning system, which brought the trains to a (3.　) stop. An earthquake sends two kinds of waves—P-waves and S-waves. The latter, the (4.　) waves, are more destructive but travel more slowly, and this time gap makes the advanced warning possible.

a. early　**b.** massive　**c.** primary　**d.** secondary　**e.** speedy

Part II   DL 57   CD2-25

The P-wave-(1.　) system is very useful, but it does not always give us enough advanced warning to prepare for a coming (2.　). If you are near the epicenter, the time difference between P-waves and S-waves is very small and S-waves might strike almost immediately after the P-waves, leaving less time on our side. We must understand the system's (3.　) and, for safety's sake, avoid active (4.　) when building high speed train lines.

a. calculation　**b.** detection　**c.** earthquake　**d.** faults　**e.** limitations

Writing Practice

日本文の意味に合った英文になるように、[　]内の語句を並べかえましょう。

1. 多くの人命を救ったのは、奇跡ではなく科学だった。

   [a miracle / but / it / not / science / that / was] saved the lives of many people.

2. 予知を与える十分な時間差があるかどうかは、震央からの距離しだいだ。

   It depends on how far you are from the epicenter whether there is [a time difference / advance / enough of / notice / to / give].

Unit 15

Abyss
生命を育む熱水噴出孔

宇宙の謎が次々と解明される中、21世紀最後のフロンティアとして調査が進む深海。中でも熱水噴出孔には多くの研究者が強い関心を寄せています。ここには、地球の初期生命誕生にかかわる手がかりが隠されているからです。科学技術の飛躍的な進歩は、猛烈な水圧と400℃にもなる高温に耐え得る機材の開発を可能にし、今、この瞬間にも驚くような事実が確認されているかもしれません。科学者が目を疑ったほどの、噴出孔周辺に息づく豊かな生態系の発見は、その一例です。

Pre-Exercises

Focus on Words　CheckLink

日本語の意味に合うようにa～f、g～lの各語群から適切な語を選びましょう。

1. 光合成の過程を見直す　　　　reconsider the (　　) of photosynthesis
2. 壁の裂け目を隠す　　　　　　hide a (　　) in the wall
3. 細菌を除去する　　　　　　　get rid of (　　)
4. オゾン層を保護する　　　　　protect the ozone (　　)
5. 怪しげな車両を監視する　　　monitor a suspicious (　　)

　　　a. bacteria　**b.** crack　**c.** layer
　　　d. process　**e.** shrimp　**f.** vehicle

6. 全人生を教育にささげる　　　dedicate an (　　) life to education
7. 地殻活動を分析する　　　　　analyze (　　) activity
8. ひどい臭いを放つ　　　　　　give off a (　　) smell
9. 活火山を探検する　　　　　　explore an (　　) volcano
10. 有人ロケットを打ち上げる　　launch a (　　) rocket

　　　g. active　**h.** entire　**i.** horrible
　　　j. independent　**k.** manned　**l.** tectonic

Reading

Part I　　　　　　　　　　　　　DL 58　　CD2-26

　　Growing up, most of us were taught that all life comes from the sun. We were taught that the sun's energy and photosynthesis, the process of transferring light energy into organic material, were needed to sustain the food chain. However, recently, scientists have discovered entire ecosystems that live completely independent of the sun and its energy. Scientists exploring the ocean depths have found ecosystems that can live on a different energy source: thermal vents.

　　Thermal vents are small holes or cracks in the surface of the planet. They look like mini-volcanoes. However, unlike volcanoes, geothermally heated water flows out from these vents into the environment. And as you might expect, these vents are usually found in geologically active areas where tectonic plates are moving apart. As a result, many of these vents are found deep under the sea on the ocean floor, at depths well beyond the reach of the sun.

　　Scientists were amazed to discover entire ecosystems around these thermal vents. Not only were there bacteria, but also communities of organisms much higher up the food chain, including tube worms, crabs, clams, shrimp and fish. Ordinarily, the deep ocean floor does not sustain much life, so scientists were surprised to find that life around these thermal vents was like a jungle, teeming with organisms.

　　Furthermore, these ecosystems have grown and developed without any energy from the sun.

Part II　　　　　　　　　　　　DL 59　　CD2-27

　　While photosynthesis powers life on the planet surface,

Notes

photosynthesis
光合成

organic material
有機物質

entire ecosystems
まとまった生態系

thermal vent
熱水噴出孔

geothermally
地熱によって

vent　噴出孔

geologically
地質学的に

tectonic plates
（地殻の）構造プレート

beyond the reach of ~
～が届かない

communities　生物群集

worms
ぜん虫（サナダムシやセンチュウのような細長く柔らかい体をした足のない下等動物の俗称）

clams　二枚貝

teeming with ~
～で満ちている

the process that sustains these deep water ecosystems is called chemosynthesis. Thermal heating vents release water that is rich in hydrogen sulfide. Hydrogen sulfide is perhaps best known to us as that horrible smell of rotten eggs that is sometimes present around naturally heated hot springs.

With chemosynthesis, bacteria are able to live on the hydrogen sulfide that comes pouring out of these thermal vents. These bacteria can create energy as the bottom layer in the food chain. In essence, they turn hydrogen sulfide into organic matter that can then be consumed by other animals, which allows a community to develop.

Thermal vents were first discovered in 1977 by a team of scientists on Alvin, a deep-sea manned research vehicle, while exploring the ocean floor near the Galapagos Islands in the Pacific.

Scientists exploring the ocean floor were surprised to find hot water, rich in minerals pouring out of these vents, and that there were many forms of life around them.

These vents are important because they give us information about how life has developed on Earth. Furthermore, and more importantly, they can also teach us about the possibility of life on other planets, elsewhere in the universe. Secrets about the universe might be found under our own oceans here on Earth.

(448 words)

▶ 熱水噴出孔は煙突のように海底からつき出していたその形から、チムニー（英語で「煙突」の意味）とも呼ばれる。

Exercises

Focus on Phrases

語群から(　　)に適切な語を入れて英文を完成させましょう。
その際、必要に応じて語形は変えること。

1. As more people have moved, the small village has (　　　　) into a town.
2. He found that the water was (　　　　) out steadily from the tank.
3. I tried to (　　　　) apart two adjoining tables and use them separately.
4. The tourists enjoyed watching the coral (　　　　) with colorful fish.
5. His gossip was (　　　　) to everyone.

> flow　　know　　teem　　transform　　move

Focus on Contents

本文の内容に合うように(　　)に適切な語句を選びましょう。

Part I

1. An ecosystem that does not depend on the sun was discovered (　　).
   a. on the volcano　**b.** in the deep sea　**c.** near the other planet
2. The discovery of (　　) around the thermal vents amazed scientists.
   a. a jungle　**b.** a food chain　**c.** many organisms

Part II

1. Bacteria play an important role around thermal vents by changing hydrogen sulfide into (　　).
   a. communities of organisms　**b.** hot springs　**c.** organic matter
2. Thermal vents enable us to collect information about (　　).
   a. the existence of unknown planets　**b.** the evidence of aliens
   c. the beginning of life on Earth

Abyss Unit 15

Summary

（　）にa〜eから適切な語を選び、それぞれのPartの要約文を作りましょう。

Part I

It is common knowledge that the source of all life on Earth comes from the sun. Light energy is transferred into organic material through the process of (1.　　). Recently, however, utterly different communities of (2.　　) have been discovered around thermal (3.　　) deep under the sea, where bacteria as well as other creatures higher up the food chain are thriving, creating a unique (4.　　) independent of the sun.

a. ecosystem **b.** organisms **c.** plates **d.** photosynthesis **e.** vents

Part II

These thermal vents (1.　　) hot water rich in hydrogen sulfide in which bacteria are able to live. Then they (2.　　) it into organic matter for other higher-level creatures to (3.　　), allowing them to form a community. Since thermal vents were first discovered in 1977, scientists have paid attention to them, as they could give us precious information about how life (4.　　) on Earth, and furthermore, on whether life is possible on other planets in the universe.

a. consume **b.** developed **c.** explore **d.** release **e.** turn

Writing Practice

日本文の意味に合った英文になるように、[　]内の語句を並べかえましょう。

1. 太陽光の届くはるか圏外の深い海底に、科学者たちはまとまった生態系を発見した。

Scientists have discovered entire ecosystems on the ocean floor [at / beyond / depths / of / the reach / the sun / well].

2. この島は、熱水孔が発見された最初の場所として、人々に最もよく知られている。

The island is [as / best / known / people / to] the first place where thermal vents were found.

```
このシールをはがすと
CheckLink 利用のための
「教科書固有番号」が
記載されています。
一度はがすと元に戻すことは
できませんのでご注意下さい。

4006
Science Matters!
```

本書には CD（別売）があります

Science Matters!
暮らしを変える最新科学

2015 年 1 月 20 日　初版第 1 刷発行
2023 年 2 月 20 日　初版第 12 刷発行

編　者　　野　﨑　嘉　信
　　　　　松　本　和　子
　　　　　Alastair Graham-Marr
　　　　　Kevin Cleary

発行者　　福　岡　正　人
発行所　　株式会社　金　星　堂
（〒101-0051）東京都千代田区神田神保町 3-21
Tel.（03）3263-3828（営業部）
　　（03）3263-3997（編集部）
Fax（03）3263-0716
https://www.kinsei-do.co.jp

編集担当　長島吉成　　　　　　　　Printed in Japan
印刷所・製本所／萩原印刷株式会社
本書の無断複製・複写は著作権法上での例外を除き禁じられています。本書を代行業者等の第三者に依頼してスキャンやデジタル化することは、たとえ個人や家庭内での利用であっても認められておりません。
落丁・乱丁本はお取り替えいたします。

ISBN978-4-7647-4006-8 C1082